gal Design Book

meier & Meera Klemola 2021

ublished in 2021.

meier & Meera Klemola

n: Tobias Heumann

-book.com

-4725-1

The Le

First edition p
by Astrid Kohl

Layout and Desi
www.legaldesign

ISBN: 978-952-94

THE LEGAL DESIGN BOOK

Doing Law
In The
21st Century

Astrid Kohlmeier
Meera Klemola

Chapters

You can use this space for notes or sketches

Introduction →

Introduction

Dear Reader,

Thank you for your curiosity and desire to learn.

We are Meera Klemola and Astrid Kohlmeier, two legal design pioneers with an aspiration to raise legal design awareness and bring legal design tools into the hands of every legal professional.

As trained lawyers and designers, we want to share with you the experiences and insights we have gained over the last years as consultants leading legal design and innovation initiatives with a broad range of clients, such as law firms, in-house legal departments, universities and institutes, and legal tech companies.

Our main goal is to support these organizations in their legal innovation activities. Both of us have led many successful and first-to-industry projects and workshops with our clients based on our individually developed concepts of legal design. Meera lives in Helsinki, Finland and Astrid close to Munich, Germany. We decided to collaborate and combine forces to write this book in order to share rich insights, use cases and expertise collectively gathered over the years working as leaders in legal design.

When reading this book, we wish for you to explore and understand:

- What the new discipline of "legal design" really is.
- How you can work with it and what you can do with it.
- How legal design is changing the way legal teams work.
- Why the next innovation level in law should be creating "intuitive legal experiences."
- Why this is all so utterly helpful for legal professionals and legal organizations today and tomorrow.

This book is indispensable for anyone who is especially interested in topics like:

- How to develop useful and engaging legal services and products for your clients.
- How to solve the right problems to create solutions that bring real added value.
- How to transform legal advice, services and products into intuitive experiences.
- How to redesign and re-systemize traditional legal work environments.
- How to establish savvy legal business units instead of cost centers.
- How to prepare for and excel in the era of (legal) digital transformation.

Our mission

With this book, we not only seek to answer the main questions around legal design and provide some tangible practical examples: we want to push it further. We focus on the opportunities legal design presents as a toolkit to make legal content and workflows simpler. We explore the future roles of the legal designer as a title and profession in the workplace. In addition, we explain the opportunities we see in what we both call "legal experiences."

We want legal matters to fit into daily professional and private lives seamlessly. Legal design is the key that leads to smooth legal experiences. In the best case scenario, the law no longer will consider itself to be a separate area of expertise, but an embedded part of products, services and processes. Law should be an intuitive part of daily routines, and should therefore be a natural part of all our new systems and technical developments. To achieve this, one first needs a mindset that is open to new solutions to gradually adapt the individual ecosystems. Step by step, this redesign approach has the potential to shape a transparent legal system in which law is not a barrier, but rather an enabler.

With legal design, you can change the way people experience the necessity of law, and we want law to become a fitting piece in the mosaic that also plays an important role in the digital transformation.

Legal design in a nutshell

Let us first begin with a very quick definition of legal design in order to open up your mind for the first chapter. Legal design is a human-centered approach to legal problem-solving and legal innovation.

> Legal design can be defined as **"design deployed in the field of law to transform legal products, services, work, systems, business strategies, ecosystems and user experience."**

It combines the lawyer's legal expertise with the designer's mindset and methodologies as well as the technological potential to create useful, useable, understandable and engaging legal outcomes for all.

People who are new to the topic might not immediately understand why such a hybrid like "legal design" could hold the magic key for the legal industry on its way to becoming a digital service industry with simple and user-centric solutions.
But no worries: we will lead you step by step and hope for your "aha!" moment by the time you finish reading this book. We have also designed a set of Legal Design Philosophies, which are guiding principles to assist you in embracing legal design. This is all set out in Chapters 1 and 2 of this book.

Why legal design? – A first overview

Why invest in legal design? As we move towards an increasingly digital world, in which the need to respond and react in a fast and dynamic manner becomes essential, it is necessary to update our ways of working. Legal design is one way of working and an innovation method that can assist legal teams to respond appropriately to changing customer needs and technological advancement. In Chapter 3, we look at some of the key challenges faced by the legal industry and why we can look to legal design as a way to combat these challenges.

How to do legal design

Chapter 4 sets out our legal design process, which will help you perform legal design within your own team. We deep dive into each "step" in the legal design process, providing clear and detailed instructions on how to run your own legal design projects. In this chapter, we also introduce you to a series of different methodologies and tools that will enable you to do legal design with integrity and obtain the best results.

Field work

We dedicate a full chapter to showcasing some of our favorite legal design projects from the field. We have included both our own projects as well as legal design initiatives carried out by others. In this chapter, you will discover the breadth of legal design's applicability and see how other legal teams have implemented legal design to create better outcomes. Our case studies include projects from Airbus, Clifford Chance and Queen Mary University, to name just a few.

The role of the legal designer

As the term "legal design" starts to become a part of the legal lexicon, we will also see a rise in recognition of the role of the legal designer within legal teams and organizations. Just as we have seen the normalizing of "legal technologists," legal designers, too, will become a natural part of legal ecosystems. What are the skills, knowledge and attributes that a legal designer must possess in order to create meaningful impact? How can one train to become a legal designer? And what are the types of roles within both inhouse teams and law firms where the legal designer might excel? This is all unpacked in Chapter 6.

Legal experiences

What constitutes a great legal experience? We introduce you to our framework for legal quality, spanning a foundation of profound legal advice, user-friendliness and intuitive legal experiences. We discuss the need to focus on creating unique legal user experiences (LUX) and encourage legal professionals to take a truly user-centered approach in order to provide users with legal solutions in an intuitive way.

Measuring the value of legal design

The final chapter in this book discusses the need for legal teams to hone the practice of setting key performance indicators and measuring the overall impact of different innovation initiatives, including legal design projects. We encourage legal professionals to start becoming comfortable with data, analytics and making data-driven decisions. This chapter provides tips on how to start collecting the right data and the types of key performance indicators (KPIs) you might like to set and measure over the course of time to determine the impact of your legal design initiatives.

A side note on legal design and access to justice

Legal design is increasingly used as a tool to design better processes that increase access to justice. We now see legal design used by courts in several countries to design a more equal and accessible legal system. The role of legal design in enhancing access to justice deserves its very own book. This book focusses primarily on how legal design is used within business contexts.

So, you're ready to explore all that legal design has to offer? Before turning the page, ask yourself these questions:

- Are you seeking to lead innovation strategies?
- Do you wish to bring clarity to complexity?
- Do you desire to connect more meaningfully with your clients?
- Do you wish to empower others to better understand the law?
- Are you looking for ways to distinguish yourself from the competition?
- Does your organization need to embrace new ways of doing business?
- Do you want to learn new skills?
- Are you seeking to collaborate more with other professionals and experts outside of law?
- Does your organization still operate within the constraints of silos?
- Do you find yourself feeling powerless to effect change within your organization?

If you answered yes to any of these questions, this book is for you!
Your legal design journey awaits.

⟵ Introduction

Chapter 1
The Legal Design Philosophies

1

The Legal Design Philosophies

The Philosophies

Defer Judgement/
Fail Fast/
Curiosity and Creativity/
The Art of Pivoting/
Focus on Objectives/
Multidisciplinary Teams/
A Seat at the Table for Everyone/
Talk to Clients and Stakeholders/
Building to Learn/
Embrace an Open Environment/

Chapter 1
The Legal Design Philosophies

In order to be a legal designer, do legal design, teach legal design and use legal design within your team, it is necessary to adopt the right mental models and create the ideal environmental conditions for design to thrive.

We have defined ten fundamental mental models, which we call the Legal Design Philosophies. In order to guarantee success for your legal design projects and initiatives, we recommend that you familiarize yourself with these Philosophies and routinely incorporate them into your work – be it at an individual level or within a team context. Guided by the Legal Design Philosophies, you will move towards creating the right culture and space for yourself and your team to build, apply, implement and ultimately benefit from legal design.

Defer judgement – of ourselves and of others.

A critical thinker with a discerning eye for mistakes – sound familiar? Yes, legal professionals are the masters of sifting through copious amounts of facts and quickly identifying the challenges, barriers and mistakes. It is skills like these that make lawyers proficient in their roles. However, it is this very same skill – the critical eye – that may limit the exploration of broader horizons and new ideas. Why? Because the default action of this mental model is to mitigate risk. Laywers tend to rationalize the pitfalls of an idea to reduce risk. Because of this tendency, we find that many ideas in legal ecosystems are often discarded before they even have the chance to incubate and flourish.

Classical legal environments do not foster creativity

The majority of lawyers work in traditional legal environments. In these traditional settings, you typically find a certain fear of failure that is firmly anchored in their occupants' DNA. This is coupled with the ideology of mitigating risk and avoiding it wherever possible. A key reason for risk adversity stems from the conditioning found in legal education and training in universities. Legal solutions are supposed to be perfect and consistent with the respective laws – and indeed, it is for such precision that lawyers are paid. Imprecise solutions come at a great cost, with severe consequences such as individual or firm liability. To avoid liability, lawyers aim to create watertight solutions. This is necessary in order (in the best case) to ensure legal certainty. Again, it is what lawyers are paid to do.

Coming from such a background, it is understandable why lawyers generally fear imperfect solutions. The idea of embracing failure as a learning tool is therefore quite an uncomfortable concept in legal ecosystems. It is important to reduce your judgement of yourself and others in order to understand what legal design – as a trial and error method – means for lawyers.

In addition, it is particularly difficult to share your creative self in a setting where you know that your idea will fall under heavy scrutiny. As a consequence, many legal ecosystems tend to become places in which ideas are not shared for fear of judgement. Legal design requires us to move away from this culture of justification and judgement and instead let thoughts, suggestions and recommendations for solutions flow freely at the outset. In order to do this, it is essential to defer judgement – not just of others, but also of yourself.

2 FAIL FAST

Do not let the fear of failure kill the potential of new trajectories.

The "F" word. Failure. If you are a legal professional, failure is one of the most feared outcomes. The thought of embracing failure as a method of learning often leaves legal professionals feeling as though they would be embracing mediocrity or borderline complacency. This is not the case at all, and legal professionals need to start shaking themselves free from this perception of failure.

Embracing failure without loss of quality

Embracing failure does not mean underperforming. It does not mean reducing the quality of your services, and it certainly does not mean providing negligent legal advice. When we talk about embracing failure, it needs to be put into context. We see it as an important vehicle for developing better solutions without diluting the security of legal advice. And it is also clear that lawyers in particular have little room for error due to their liability. This is certainly an important reason why many lawyers have so far shied away from new possibilities.

However, if we are talking about client service transformation and defining a new standard of legal advice, products and services, then this does require us to experiment and try new things. Some of these trials and experiments may not produce the results you anticipated – that is, they will fail. Too often, however, we observe that legal professionals (and the organizations in which they work) let the fear of failure (and the misconception that it would lead to a loss in reputation or credibility) stop them from even assessing new possibilities or trajectories.

Instead, legal professionals should learn to embrace failure as an important milestone in the innovation and change process. Each time you try a new idea and it does not succeed, you need to use this as a learning activity. What worked and why? What didn't work and why? Where could you improve for next time? It is important to fail quickly, learn quickly and keep moving forward with innovation. Legal design embraces the designer's motto of "fail fast and often," making a case for quick experimentation as a way to learn and identify new possibilities for the industry.

Be curious; unleash your own creativity and the creativity of others!

When people are asked what skills describe a designer, the answer is usually that designers are, above all, very creative.

Creativity is certainly a basic skill that designers must possess in order to develop new ideas. If you ask other professionals, like lawyers in particular, whether they consider themselves creative, the majority will usually answer no. This is indeed a phenomenon that needs to be examined more closely.

Children have the key to creativity

Countless studies confirm that as children we are blessed with free creativity because we can initially move around predominantly free of rules and boundaries. This applies both to our mobility and to our ability to let our imaginations run free. Regardless of whether this creativity is expressed through painting, storytelling or imaginative dance figures, children are usually not afraid of being embarrassed and giving free rein to their desire to discover and try things out. At the latest when we enter school this behavior changes, and our naturally free-thinking minds suddenly have to learn to deal with topics such as logic and diligence. The free play of the child is suppressed, and thus their creative abilities are gradually restricted.

Creativity is thus usually perceived as a hindrance in school and university education. Especially when we look into one of the most logical and analytical areas of study, jurisprudence, it becomes clear that creative abilities are not particularly emphasized or taught here. It is particularly required that the relevant jurisdiction is applied precisely and follows a certain pattern. Law schools often teach law students how to structure answers in an "ideal way." In this context, the word "creative" is not one that is usually associated with "a good lawyer."

Creativity meets rationality

But legal design is the opposite of fixed patterns and procedures. It is about creating innovations and new solutions. And for new ideas we need creativity. The big question is how we can revive this hidden ability. How can we (re)build our "creative confidence"?[1] The good thing is that creativity can be relearned and even increased with the right mental exercises! In their book, *The Secret of the Highly Creative Thinker*, Dorte Nielsen and Sarah Thurber reveal that one of the core skills that foster creative ideas is the ability to make unexpected connections and see combinations others do not see.[2] And making those connections can be trained regularly to improve your capacity to think creatively.

Rediscover your creative flow

Legal design projects use specific creativity techniques that help lawyers rediscover their inner children and get back to the creative power that is inherent in each of us. To get into the state of creative flow, the mental and physical conditions first need to be set. We have included some tips for setting up innovative physical spaces[3] at the end of this chapter.

We would like to encourage you to rediscover your roots and get back to your creative nature. Especially in the beginning, people often find it difficult to describe ideas using simple drawings, for example. But our experience

---

1 Kelley and Kelley, *Creative Confidence*

2 Nielsen and Thurber, *The Secret of the Highly Creative Thinker*, 17

3 "If you look at history innovation doesn't come just from giving people incentives; it comes from creating environments where their ideas can connect." "Kevin Kelly and Steven Johnson on Where Ideas Come From." www.wired.com. September 27, 2010.

shows that it is worthwhile to take part in this experiment and invest the time to rediscover your creative capabilities. You will see how much fun it is to have a creative ideation session with your colleagues (and even clients!) and to lure yourself and others out of their usual thinking patterns. Shared creativity is an especially unifying force that can weld you and your team together.

4 THE ART OF PIVOTING

Do not fall in love with your ideas. Observe client behavior and be ready to pivot.

YouTube, Slack, Shopify and Yelp. Aside from being some of the most notable global companies, what else do they have in common? The answer is: the pivot. Each of these companies has successfully pivoted from its initial business model, product and value proposition to create the giant brands that we all know and use today.

In the realm of business, a pivot, or "pivoting," is commonplace. It refers to a change in business trajectory, usually inspired by noteworthy consumer behavior. Pivoting is not common in legal business. If it were, most law firms would have observed consumer trends towards digitization and digitalization and focused a large portion of their resources on building their connected services offering to grow a new, more scalable and automated revenue stream at least a decade ago. One reason law firms have failed to pivot or quickly adapt to changing client trends in the market is because they rarely commit resources to a vital function called experience design.

Law firms need experience design functions

The most successful and iconic global players, like Apple, PepsiCo and Proctor & Gamble (P&G), invest in design. They invest in design not just in terms of form and aesthetics, but also in terms of strategy. Experience design is a crucial aspect of designing any successful product or service.

Experience designers focus on observing client behavior, understanding what drives client decision-making and providing the client voice to internal decision-making processes. In the design teams at iconic companies, you will not only find user experience (UX) designers, industrial designers, illustrators and animators, you will also find people who work on experience design. These experts bring skills such as strategic design, design research, psychology, ethnography and explicit education in human-centered design to the organization.

Innovative law firms still tend to focus mainly on tech

We have encountered some advanced law firms that have appointed innovation heads or created innovation teams, but their task is usually focused on technological advancement within the firm. Who is taking care of designing the legal experience? We advocate that law firms should not only appoint innovation and tech teams, but also form experience design teams to champion truly client-centric strategies.

The experience design team's purpose is to holistically assess the ecosystem and represent the voice of the client to ensure that every piece of technology created by the legal tech team, or every new initiative founded by the innovation team, or every business strategy decided on by management is aligned with client needs, motivations and expectations. This ensures that the legal firm is making informed decisions aligned with both client preferences and business goals. It also enables legal businesses to quickly assess whether a pivot is required, spot new trends and introduce new revenue streams to their existing services ahead of client requests.

An experience design function will help legal firms transform from being reactive players in the market to proactive market leaders.
We discuss this more in Chapter 7: Legal User Experience.

Pivoting in the context of legal design

Let's come back to the pivot. In legal design, the word "pivot" refers to changing the trajectory of ideas or proposed solutions based on observations of client behavior. To pivot in legal design means to let go of an old idea and embrace a new direction, which often presents itself after spending time learning what actions would truly assist clients (internal or external) in achieving their goals. In legal design, pivoting does not necessarily mean changing the goal; in fact, the goal often stays the same. What changes is the path, approach or solution you implement to reach it.

Flexibility is a success factor

To highlight the importance of being open to pivoting, let's take a closer look at the global online review platform Yelp. Today, in the United States in particular, the ability for a local business to thrive is heavily influenced by the support it garners from the local community in the form of Yelp reviews. But believe it or not, Yelp was not always the successful referral and review platform it is today. It was originally founded as an automated system that allowed users to ask friends for direct recommendations – an idea that did not take off with audiences as intended. Nevertheless, while analyzing user feedback and behavior, the founders noticed interesting patterns. They discovered that customers were using the original Yelp platform to write reviews of local businesses, and they were doing this just for fun. The founders quickly pivoted, abandoning *their* original idea and instead following a new, customer-informed direction. Since then, Yelp has grown to be one of the largest and most trusted review and referral platforms, with approximately 170 million unique visits to the site each month and over 150 million independent reviews.

Now, where do you think Yelp would be today if its founders had not been open to pivoting and instead had been fixated on realizing their own idea and vision for what the company should be (irrespective of what customer evidence suggested)?

Let ideas flow and grow

So remember that when it comes to legal design, it is important that you do not allow yourself to become fixated on an idea to the extent that you fail to recognize important cues from clients indicating that a different idea, approach or solution would better suit their needs. Always be prepared to pivot.

5 FOCUS ON OBJECTIVES

Set clear objectives and performance targets from the outset and continuously refer back to these objectives in order to stay on target.

A common misconception is that legal design is "touchy feely" and lacks concrete direction. The best legal design initiatives are highly focused. From the outset, the team should list and familiarize themselves with the objectives of the initiative and establish a "what constitutes success" (WCS) statement. Without clear, well-defined objectives and a WCS statement, it is easy to veer off course. Even worse, it is easy to lose individuals along the way as they start to forget the real purpose of the legal design project and what they are trying to achieve. For the project leader, it is important to constantly ensure that the team does not lose sight of the objectives. Objectives and goals should be referred to regularly and used as an anchor to guide the team on the right path. Chapter 8 will provide you with tips on how to set the right key performance indicators (KPIs) to measure your success and the value of legal design.

6 MULTIDISCIPLINARY TEAMS

Legal design teams should comprise professionals from various disciplines.

Legal design works on the premise that perhaps the most powerful contributions and changes in law can be made possible when legal problems are not tasked to lawyers alone to solve, but instead are assigned to a variety of professionals, combining their various areas of expertise. Traditionally, lawyers perceive their colleagues as either lawyers or "non-lawyers." The lawyers in a law firm are perceived as fee earners and the other professionals as "fee burners."

This seemingly innocent delineation between lawyers and other professionals who work in law firms has serious ramifications for creating multidisciplinary teams, because it positions a lawyer's contribution as more valuable than that of another professional. We have observed that this type of delineation gives lawyers a false sense of elitism, which is not conducive to collaborative, multidisciplinary work – particularly as we move into a digital economy. When we look at other professions, this behavior of categorizing professionals as "A" or "non-A" is not the norm. For example, a doctor does not refer to nurses as "non-doctors" or to medical receptionists as "non-doctor professionals," so why does the legal system insist on referring to other professionals as "non-lawyers"? We believe that such categorizing of people is not only outdated, but it does not reflect the modern values of society in 2021, particularly those of the Millennial generations and younger, who embrace differences and are not so concerned with labels, titles and pigeonholing people into single categories. We should conduct ourselves with integrity and respect for everyone's expertise, and that means giving professionals with different sets of skills the respect and recognition they deserve.

The educated lone warrior

One reason for this phenomenon of categorization lies, once again, in legal education. In universities, lawyers are educated to be lone warriors. They do not learn what the advantages might be of joining forces with other lawyers or even with other professionals. The added value that multidisciplinary work creates is simply unknown to most lawyers. The legal curriculum generally refers to the respective substantive laws and, if necessary, how they can best be enforced through a lawyer's professional work. The emphasis is on students' knowledge of the subject matter and how well they can apply the forms of the respective laws. This one-sided way of thinking does not prepare students for the challenges of the practical working world. We see an urgent need for reforms and updates to legal education and advocate that law schools should be equipping their future law students with legal design skills in order to ensure that they thrive in today's workplace. Between the two of us, we have co-taught legal design modules with professors at various universities, and we have witnessed firsthand the change in mindset towards collaboration and client-centricity and the creativity it brings about in law students.

For legal professionals working "in-house" at companies or organizations, the story is a little different. Within an organizational context, lawyers working in-house are generally viewed as cost centers, while their counterparts in marketing, product development and business functions are viewed as contributors to the bottom line. In-house lawyers are often unfairly perceived as a hindrance to business as opposed to being facilitators.

Whichever scenario we look at – be it in a law school, a law firm or in an organization – it appears that the legal function is often siloed off from other professions, making it more difficult to reap the benefits of multidisciplinary working.

Today we are moving towards client-centric, connected solutions and as such, distinctions between lawyers and "non-lawyers" are becoming less relevant. To create connected service solutions, you need to bring lawyers' expertise together with technical expertise for building, design expertise for user and client experience, marketing expertise to boost brand awareness and sales expertise for conversion. All of these experts are thus becoming part of the same value proposition, and each is no more important than the other in the value chain. Therefore, in the new world where legal services are moving more toward connected services, the lawyer is not necessarily at the center, but instead is a key component together with their contemporaries from other professional backgrounds.

In addition to the business need for multidisciplinary teams is the fact that the ability to innovate and disrupt increases in multidisciplinary teams. We see this as a huge benefit when operating in a highly competitive market such as the legal profession.

Legal design is diverse, inclusive and gives everyone a seat at the table.

Legal design is democratic and inclusive. It thrives when there is diversity in the room, bringing together people who may differ in age, race, religion, gender or expertise to name a few. Every voice counts – and especially at the idea generation phase, no voice has more or less clout than another. Legal design requires everyone's active engagement and participation.

Legal design often uses brainstorming sessions and constructive criticism to weed out the best and worst ideas or solutions to a problem. These sessions are usually led by an experienced facilitator who understands the importance of ensuring that every voice in the room is heard.

This process means that you generate a large pool of ideas and then, as a team, rally behind the *best* idea once you have it – no matter whether it comes from the most distinguished lawyer in the room or from the newest recruit.

Often companies in the corporate world don't think this way; they are hierarchical or siloed into expertise, which prevents innovative change and progress. The core tenet of legal design – that ideas are more important than stature or expertise – is fundamental. As legal design becomes an integral part of "lawyering," we see legal design as a way of increasing diversity, reducing hierarchies and enhancing democracy within law.

Start asking better questions, and include your clients in the process.

In order to design the right things, you need to ask the right questions from the right people. Sounds simple, doesn't it? And yet, the legal industry so often shies away from doing just this. Why? For most lawyers, the thought of inviting clients to ask *them* questions feels counterintuitive. Lawyers are used to playing the role of the "solution provider" or "answer-giver." Doubts creep in: "What will my client think if I now ask them for their input?" The answer is: they will be grateful. Your clients will feel grateful, heard and more often than not, excited to co-create solutions that will actively assist their business and its operations. So often we have heard our in-house clients request that their law firms would pick up the phone and speak to them: ask them what their everyday challenges are; ask them what their key performance indicators (KPIs) are this year; ask them about their overarching goals and priorities so they can make better use of everyone's time and money. Working *with* clients also fosters stronger relationships between all those involved, leading to enduring business relationships.

Including clients, stakeholders and end users from the outset and asking them questions is one of the most important steps toward achieving client-centricity. Without client and stakeholder input, innovation directions and decisions that you make will be based on assumptions as opposed to first hand evidence, which can lead you to develop solutions that are not really desired or useful. So, as you continue your journey toward practicing legal design, get comfortable reaching out to your clients, stakeholders and end users and involving them as you create new solutions.

9 BUILDING TO LEARN

Build to learn.

Think back to when you were a child. You will most likely have some memories of trying to build something, whether it was a treehouse, a Lego tower, a papier-mâché ball or a vision in your head that you wanted to make tangible. Children experiment and build everyday – it's how we learn.

As lawyers embark on the journey to become legal professionals, through university and their time in the workplace, there is little opportunity to continue building to learn. Legal education focuses on the past, on precedents and rote learning. As you move through the legal workplace, you may occasionally use small diagrams – to depict transactions, for example – but otherwise, it is always words that lawyers use to make their ideas tangible. A prime example is in legal textbooks, which are filled with words and descriptions of what a contract ought to look like or include. However, they rarely include pictures of contracts, downloadable templates or resources, business model diagrams for running a law firm, "pop-up" interactive learning labs or any number of other tools. Lawyers do not create and are not taught to create 'legal artefacts' – that is, tangible expressions (outside the realm of words) for modelling possible solutions and progressions in the law.

The traditional legal mindset is reactive.

One reason for this avoidance of building to learn could be the mindset that lawyers have been taught to adopt in terms of innovation: that is, a reactive mindset rather than a proactive one. If we look at substantive legal innovation, it is most often in response to a new law or a client demand. There is very little prospective innovation and research. In other words, the legal culture is not one that promotes building to learn. The idea that experimenting and building purely with the view to discover what might be possible is not inherent in the legal field. There is not the same attitude toward fostering research and development that we observe in other industries, which see dollars invested in prospective research as valuable and necessary in order to continuously push barriers and redefine frontiers.

Legal design embodies the notion of building to learn. Creating tangible concepts of ideas and taking a proactive approach to innovation is essential. It is not necessary to create minimum viable products that require heavy capital investment; they can be scrappy prototypes, drawings or wire frames put together to model ideas and make them visible. The goal is to learn.

10 EMBRACE AN OPEN ENVIRONMENT

Establish an environment that is open for idea generation by cultivating psychological safety.

An open environment is crucial to legal design. What do we mean when we say “open environment”? There are a few elements to this. “Open” means open to new ideas, new ways of working, new ways of doing, new ways of being and new understandings of what it means to be professional.

In order for such an open environment to be created, there needs to be high levels of trust among team members. To establish such high levels of trust, there needs to be something called psychological safety.

Psychological safety in a team can be described as "a shared belief that the team is safe for interpersonal risk-taking"[4] – meaning that individuals are not afraid that they will be humiliated or punished for their words and actions. In 2015, Google concluded a study[5] on the building blocks of a successful Google team, finding that psychological safety is the prerequisite for all other factors that contribute to a high-performing team. Without psychological safety, team members will not trust the team environment enough to contribute. Consequently, psychological safety also fosters diverse ideas.

Since a key component of legal design is the creation and sharing of ideas and solutions, it is necessary for those leading legal design initiatives to establish an open environment that is psychologically safe from the outset.

To be clear, psychological safety does not mean "being nice." Rather, it relates to establishing an environment in which:

- People are encouraged to share their thoughts.
- People do not fear humiliation, judgement or loss of credibility for sharing their ideas.
- People feel comfortable giving constructive criticism to their peers.
- People feel comfortable receiving constructive criticism from their peers.

Psychological safety cannot be faked. People can intuit from leaders whether an environment is *really* open or not. Psychological safety must be advocated and practiced by leadership in order for a team to establish real trust in one another.

4 Edmonson, "Psychological Safety," 6

5 Rozovsky, "The five keys to a successful Google team"

I need results. Yesterday!
Can't we just talk for a minute?
Thanks for the input, Linda!
Yes, but did anyone look at section 2?
I don't like where this is going.

The Five Pitfalls of Legal Innovation Labs

At this point, we think it is also worth mentioning the impact that a **physical space** can have on the performance of a team practicing legal design. While it's not necessary to have state-of-the-art equipment or a Silicon Valley start-up fitout, a space should be set up in a way that facilitates collaboration, movement and experimentation. Legal innovation labs have recently popped up in many law firms; however, we have noticed that there is still room for these labs to improve their setups and create the ideal conditions for legal design work and innovation more generally.

Here is a list of five pitfalls of legal innovation labs

Focusing only on legal tech solutions and designing the room filled with fancy desktops.

Failing to identify a clear strategic vision of what you want to achieve in your space.

Corporate-branded innovation rooms: these tend focus too much on brand and external perception instead of on what people need to feel good, open-minded and comfortable creating new ideas.

Perfection over “factory” feeling.

Rooms that lack the human touch.

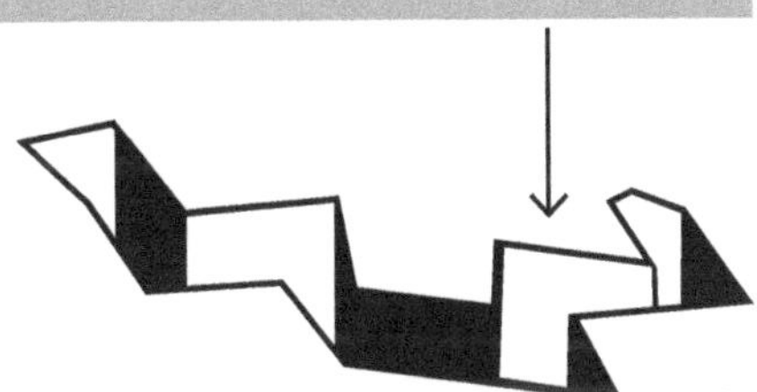

Build a Culture of True Collaboration

Transforming the culture of any organization is never an easy task. However, it is extremely important in order to ensure that legal design can reach its potential for your team and business. The design of the environment in which legal professionals and those working in the legal sector operate is every bit as important as the work produced. Do not underestimate the power of optimal conditions. The right environment (both psychologically and physically) has the power to enable employees to seize opportunities when and where they see them – and giving them the tools to create unscripted experiences is an essential element of this kind of environmental transformation.

Legal Design is not a matter of age!

Based on the ten Legal Design Philosophies you have now read, you should understand that a core aspect of legal design is multidisciplinarity. What this means is that legal design encourages legal teams to tap into the collective genius of various experts from various fields, various backgrounds – and of course, various generations – to drive change, solve problems and create solutions.

At present we have four generations in the workplace: the Baby Boomers, Generation X, Millennials – and finally at graduate level we have Gen Z, the digital natives, along with the last of the Millennials. What an opportunity this presents to explore the ideas, experience and know-how of these different generations (who view the world from such different perspectives) to create radical change within the profession!

One question that is frequently asked is whether a person's ability to do legal design is directly related to their age. The assumption is that older generations may find the mental models and ways of operating in legal design less intuitive than their younger peers do. This is a question that tends to be quite specific to the legal industry, where hierarchical attitudes flourish. There are not too many other industries (except perhaps academia and medicine) in which a person's age directly correlates to seniority and standing within an organization. It makes sense, then, that the question of age would arise in the context of legal design, too.

Interestingly, we have found that age is not a barrier to doing legal design. In our workshops and projects, we have encountered young professionals who are less comfortable with collaborative, multidisciplinary work environments than their peers in older age groups – and vice versa. What this indicates is that an ability to adopt legal design in one's own practice is not a matter of age, but rather a matter of mindset and willingness to accept new possibilities. It comes down to an individual's propensity to embrace change, challenge existing thought patterns and adopt new ways of working.

The 10 Legal Design Philosophies

1 Defer Judgement

Defer judgement – of ourselves and of others.

2 Fail Fast

Do not let the fear of failure kill the potential of new trajectories.

3 Curiosity and Creativity

Be curious; unleash your own creativity and the creativity of others!

4 The Art of Pivoting

Do not fall in love with your ideas. Observe client behavior and be ready to pivot.

5 Focus on Objectives

Set clear objectives and performance targets from the outset and continuously refer back to these objectives in order to stay on target.

6 Multidisciplinary Teams

Legal design teams should comprise professionals from various disciplines.

7 A Seat at the Table for Everyone

Legal design is diverse, inclusive and gives everyone a seat at the table.

8 Talk to Clients and Stakeholders

Start asking better questions, and include your clients in the process.

9 Building to Learn

Build to learn.

10 Embrace an Open Environment

Establish an environment that is open for idea generation by cultivating psychological safety.

Chapter 1
The Legal Design Philosophies

Chapter 2
What is Legal Design?

2

What is Legal Design?

Chapter 2
What is Legal Design?

A Brief History

Research investigating the influence and impact of design in the legal sector is very limited. To date, only a handful of academic literature has been published on this subject – compared to other industries such as healthcare, in which a plethora of research has been dedicated to identifying the strategic value design brings to that industry. Over the last four to five years, we have started to observe greater discourse on the role of design in law.

Nevertheless, according to a presentation by Stefania Passera and Helena Haapio at the Legal Design Geek Conference in 2018,[6] a few minor design influences can be observed, scattered over the past 60 years.

In the United States, the movement towards plain-language legal writing began with the 1963 book *The Language of the Law* by David Mellinkoff.[7] Plain-language science can be placed within the field of communication design, but it is equally well categorized within linguistics. A stronger influence of design in law can also be seen in the 1970s, with the emergence of "information design." However, the advent of this science did not bring about a real change in the way legal content is formulated and presented.

6 https://www.legalgeek.co. The Legal Geek is a UK-based organization for events with a focus on legal innovation and especially legal tech. In 2018 they organized a first-ever one-day event for legal design topics with more than 600 participants. Stefania Passera is a legal designer based in Helsinki; she is one of the pioneers in the field of contract design together with Helena Haapio, a lawyer and academic who is also a pioneer in the field of legal design.

7 David Mellinkoff was a professor at the UCLA School of Law and is the author of The Languge of the Law, in which he leads readers through the history of how language has been used in common law jurisdictions. He has called the law "a profession of words."

Even today, many legal texts and services are still prepared in the same way as they were 60 years ago, except that telephone and face-to-face meetings have been replaced by email. In recent years (and even more so since 2020 with the emergence of the COVID-19 pandemic) we have seen more legal communication via video calls and the use of data rooms. But this is not really connected to design or innovation itself; it is more an evolution of tech, the adoption of which was spurred by a *force majeure* situation like a pandemic.

The word combination "legal design" itself first appeared in a dissertation by Dr. Colette R. Brunschwig in 2001.[8] The influence of design on the legal profession gained greater visibility in 2013, when Stefania Passera, Margaret Hagan and Helena Haapio first employed the new term "legal design" at a "Legal Design Jam," a joint event held at Stanford University in California.[9] For the purpose of this book, we choose to define 2013 as a first milestone in the short history of legal design as we understand it today.

8 Brunschwig, Visualisierung von Rechtsnormen. Dr. Colette R. Brunschwig is a professor at the University of Zurich and is responsible for its Legal Visualizations Unit. She has published numerous books and articles about visualization in the legal field and is a visionary who writes about new concepts such as "multisensory legal education."

9 http://legaldesignjam.com/

Legal design can be defined as **"design deployed in the field of law to transform legal products, services, work, systems, business strategies, ecosystems and user experience."**

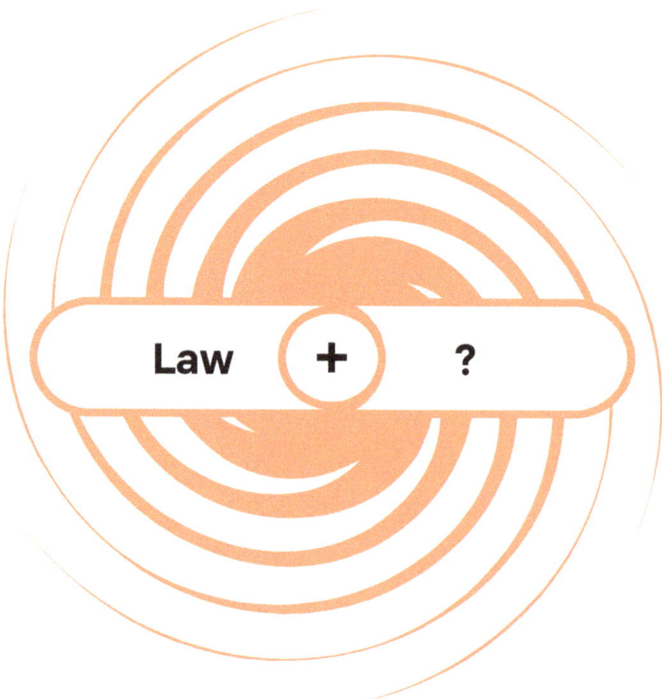

What is design?

So, if legal design is "design deployed in the field of law," what exactly is design? Let's break this down further. In order to appreciate the definition of legal design, we first need to take a step back and dive deeper into the meaning of "design." Design is multifaceted. Here we will discuss these many facets of design:

- Design as a function and theory of form
- Design as a mindset
- Design as a skill set
- Design as a process

Design as a function and theory of form

"Design is what links creativity and innovation. It shapes ideas to become practical and attractive propositions for users or customers. Design may be described as creativity deployed to a specific end."[10] – Cox Review of Creativity in Business 2005

Form follows function

When we talk about design, one of the most important principles in design theory should not go unmentioned – the idea that "form follows function."

The oft-quoted sentence "form follows function" originated with the architect Louis H. Sullivan in his essay "The Tall Office Building Artistically

10 Cox, Cox Review, 2

Considered," published in 1896. The basic idea behind it was that a skyscraper's exterior design should reflect the internal functions of the building. Sullivan attributes this thesis to nature, in which "all things have a form." This form – and by that Sullivan means the shape and external appearance of the end product (whether it be a building or the physical form of anything) – clearly reflects and intuitively communicates to us what the function of the end product is. In summary, Sullivan means that forms express the "inner life" of the objects.

This idea could be explored in the construction of typical skyscrapers, which have common interior areas designed according to their function, but also underground mechanical utility rooms, commercial areas on the lower floors, offices on the middle floor and an upper attic area generally used for storage and ventilation. However, this initially attractive idea later came under criticism because it contributed to "dehumanization." Sullivan himself expressed this in the article mentioned above: "...an unspecified number of floors of offices stacked floor by floor, one floor like another, an office like all other offices, an office like a cell in a honeycomb, just a compartment, nothing more."[11]

The fundamental considerations of the theory that "form follows function" have accompanied the design world ever since, and there are different views on the interpretation and expression of this thought. The strict interpretation of the "form follows function" principle even led to criticism of any ornament in architecture. The rejection of ornamentation and the reduction of forms to their function and thus to the essentials were then fundamental anchors for the ideas of the Bauhaus movement.

---

11 Sullivan, The Tall Office Building. The essay is accessible online at https://www.pca-stream.com/en/articles/the-tall-office-building-artistically-considered-48.

The Bauhaus

If we take a historical look at the field of design, we cannot overlook the Bauhaus, a German art school that was operational from 1919 to 1933. According to Bauhaus philosophy, design is the result of a mutual collaboration between craftsmanship and the fine arts in order to unite the principles of mass production with individual artistic vision and to combine aesthetics with everyday function.

The Bauhaus was thus not only a movement that was based on collaboration and interdisciplinarity, but its results also had an impact on everyday buildings and products. The movement also highlighted the idea that design should no longer focus solely on art, but rather on its benefit to people as part of a society that has to cope with everyday issues.

Designers' impact on society

The understanding of design at the Bauhaus school presented new artist-craftspersons (whom we would nowadays call "designers") with a comprehensive design task. Designers were not only to create everyday objects, but to also play an active role in reshaping society. According to the Bauhaus understanding of design, this term therefore referred not only to product design but also to a way of thinking and to an approach to society.

In contrast to styling, which refers to the beautification of the surface appearance of objects, design aimed to improve everyday life by providing innovative solutions for objects, systems and structures. Designers both then and today have had the task of analyzing the present and making use of their profound knowledge of the past to develop such innovative solutions for the future. They thereby develop a deep understanding of very specific contemporary questions as well as of the social, economic, political and cultural context of their time. Therefore, dealing with society, economics, politics and history influences the designer just as much as a preoccupation with art, craft and technology.[12]

This social aspect of the Bauhaus philosophy is a beautiful bridge that we can use to also locate design in law and define its benefits for society more effectively.

When we think about new concepts for better "access to justice" or "access to law," we need these and other social aspects as a solid anchor. We even claim that design holds an important key to how we can address the problem of lack of access to law worldwide. By applying the various design disciplines that we list below, we can make law truly more accessible and transparent. What can help us here are the characteristics of a human-centered design approach and the appropriate means of communication design (such as visualizations). Through visualizations and useful interactions between law and human beings based on the user's needs, we can succeed in making law more easily accessible for more people. Legal design is thus an important parameter that helps people to make better and more autonomous decisions based on their knowledge of the law.

Design as a mindset

Generally, when most people think of design, they think of aesthetics: the way something looks to the eye and feels in the hand. You might think of objects like sunglasses, vases, cars or utensils, for example. While this aspect and understanding of design is correct, it is not the full picture.

Design comes with its own unique mindset and way of viewing problems.

12 "Bauhaus #itsalldesign," an exhibition celebrating 100 years of the Bauhaus movement, March 14–December 2019, Copenhagen, Design Museum Danmark.

Essential to the design mindset is a focus on engaging people throughout the process of developing solutions for them. Every problem identified or challenge to be solved is done so through what is called a "human-centered" lens. In practice, this means that every challenge is viewed from the multiple perspectives of stakeholders or end users who will be using or interacting with the final result, no matter whether this is a product, a service or a process.

As a hypothetical example, let's imagine that you wanted to redesign the compliance training in an organization. You've noticed that employees in your organization find compliance tedious and difficult to understand, and as a result they are unknowingly breaching some of their compliance obligations on an almost routine basis.

Lawyers and designers approach tasks differently.

Generally, a lawyer's mindset is solution-focused, so you may instinctively find yourself thinking of solutions from the outset. A designer's mindset, on the other hand, is *user-focused* or *human-centered.* The mindset of a designer is such that before coming up with any solution, they will first think about those who will be reading about or interacting with compliance training. How does understanding compliance obligations impact these users on a day-to-day basis? Which parts of compliance are essential for the users to understand? Which parts are difficult to understand? How can users best comprehend and digest information? Only when the designer is equipped with such knowledge will they turn their mind to developing a solution informed by the users' responses. A designer does not presume to know the right solution without first understanding the people and the context through a human-centered lens.

Lawyers are trained to present perfect legal solutions.

Contrast the designer's approach to the intuitive response of a non-designer (such as a lawyer). More often than not, a lawyer will go straight to providing the audience with a solution, without necessarily consulting them. Lawyers tend to create solutions based on the logic of their respective jurisdictions and their own understanding of a situation. That is, they look at a problem through their own lens, as opposed to through the eyes of the person who will be using the solution. Lawyers then tend to spend time trying to provide clients with advice or convincing clients that their solution is the right one. Lawyers are trained to develop correct legal solutions that best suit their clients' goals. But their training is one-dimensional in the sense that they learn to view problems from their perspective and are not taught to provide solutions and advice in a way that makes sense from the client's point of view.

Taking this human-centered approach and stepping into the shoes of your clients may sound more tedious, especially when you are time-deprived. However, lawyers, should look at this use of time as an investment. What you will find is that by investing that initial amount of time to understand your stakeholders and end users, you will learn important information that will assist you in creating the *right* solution, which will truly bring about impactful results. The need to then *persuade* your client of the feasibility of your solution becomes significantly reduced, since the solution has been informed by user response and feedback.

Making the connection to legal design

We advocate that the designer's mindset is one of *the most important* aspects of legal design. Before starting any legal design initiative, you must first ensure that you and your team have embraced a designer's mindset – a mindset that is focused on understanding those you serve, interacting with those you serve in a two-way dialogue, exchanging thoughts and working *with* those for whom you are trying to improve your services. This mindset is key not only to identifying the right solutions and designing those solutions correctly, but also to fostering authentic relationships with stakeholders that are based on mutual respect and understanding.

Design as a skill set

Now that you have an understanding of design as a mindset, let's introduce you to the notion of design as a skill set.

During our time working at the intersection of design and law, we have observed that legal professionals often have difficulty navigating the diversity of design skills and titles. It makes sense, after all: these skills and titles are foreign to most lawyers. The result is a tendency to think that a "designer" is a person with an infinite range of skills – someone who can create visuals, make furniture, products, services, websites ...the list goes on. Making this assumption can be likened to a person believing that a "lawyer" is someone who knows about every area of the law – family, criminal, corporate, maritime, etc. You see, much like the way law is divided into different practice areas, so too is design. And when we talk about legal design, we are referring to each of the different "practice areas" (i.e., skill sets) of design being deployed to create change in law.

Overlaps between law and design

In this respect, design is not so different from law with its many different specializations. Just as legal professionals embody a basic understanding of legal practice, designers possess common knowledge in creative problem solving, visual thinking and building things.

We have observed a general uncertainty and confusion among legal professionals about which design skills are needed to address and solve particular legal challenges. For example, lawyers may not know which design skills are required:

⟶ To make legal documentation easier to understand and business-effective.

⟶ To create a legal justice system that is accessible to people who do not speak the native language.

- To assist someone in understanding their rights as a tenant.
- To develop a seamless and effective digital arbitration experience.

Each of the above situations is a legal challenge that can be solved through legal design. It is just a matter of understanding which design skill sets are required to solve each problem. Depending on your legal challenge or project, you will likely need to collaborate with one or more legal designers and perhaps a technologist, who can assist your team in navigating the entire design process and creating a design for a specific project need (e.g., redesigning compliance training, developing a new digital app to assist children going through juvenile court proceedings, etc.).

No expertise without training

Just like a specialization in law, every specialization within design requires training and expertise honed over years of practice in the field. In the same way that it would be uncommon for a lawyer to be a specialist in more than two to three areas of law, it is uncommon for designers to be specialized in numerous design skill sets. Between us (Astrid and Meera), we are trained and specialized in experience design, service design, systems design, business design, organizational design and information architecture.

Below are some of the common design skill sets that are deployed in legal design. We have broken these down into what we call "invisible design skill sets" and "tangible design skill sets." Interestingly, designers who specialize in "tangible" design skill sets are not automatically skilled at "invisible" design skill sets, and vice versa.

Thinking and acting like a designer requires specific knowledge and training. Combining the practical knowledge of law with a deep understanding of design is the magical formula for making a legal designer.

Invisible design skill sets

We refer to the following design skill sets as "invisible" design skill sets. The reason for this is that these design capabilities and the value they bring are often invisible. You will not see their outcomes in a tangible form, and yet they are crucial to creating solutions and business strategies that are client-centric. We have observed that invisible design skill sets are often disregarded by legal professionals, primarily because the value they bring is not immediately recognizable, or because legal professionals have not been educated to understand that such knowledge is actually a trained competency.

Experience design (XD): XD focuses on ensuring that the user has the best possible experience when interacting with a service, product, platform or environment. It is the practice of designing products, processes, services, events and environments with a focus on the quality of the user's experience, particularly the level of engagement and satisfaction that the user derives from each touchpoint in the process. Experience designers are holistic problem-solvers who build an understanding of an entire ecosystem – stakeholders, value creation cycles, business models and users. They are often seasoned systems thinkers, and they use this skill concurrently with human-centered design philosophies. A good experience designer is particularly skilled at conducting design research, asking good questions and facilitating workshops, focus groups and interviews. They are good at identifying patterns in user behavior, non-verbal cues and user responses to quickly iron out kinks and enhance the overall user experience.

Making the connection to legal design

We advocate that XD is at the center of legal design. Today, we live in a world in which there is immense competition and choice. The deciding factor comes down to experience. As we like to say, the best experience wins. It's as simple as that.

We encourage all people seeking to create a more usable and engaging legal environment to place experience design at the center of any innovation strategy. That way you will not only design the right solutions, but also design those solutions right. The inclusion of experience designers also aligns with our suggestion (later in the book) for legal teams to have an "experience design" board or team that is dedicated to representing the client voice.

Service design involves the activity of planning and organizing people, infrastructure, communications and the material components of a service in order to improve its value, convenience and the interaction between service providers and customers. Service design emerged out of the private sector, with a strong focus on certain service industries such as hospitality and health. Service design has been adopted widely in several jurisdictions, notably in Singapore and the UK, where each of these governments has applied service design principles to both healthcare and policy to make these systems user friendly at each touchpoint.

Making the connection to legal design

The core of almost all legal systems is the provision of services. Training programs would be well advised to place the teaching of service design at the heart of legal design education, because there is a lot that can be changed and improved through it. The great thing is that there is so much experience to draw on from other industries. Part of the art of legal design, therefore, is understanding how to develop services in other areas or industries and transferring this knowledge to legal design. Curiosity and openness, as well as the ability to apply service design to the legal world, should be key drivers for any legal designer.

Communication design focuses on the design of strategic communication and engagement with an audience. This is the process of designing how a message is delivered through a variety of channels in a consistent and engaging way. For example, a communication designer may develop a strategy for social media content. The output will likely be a series of visual or verbal "posts," which are created by a visual designer, but the strategy of when to post, how to post, what channels to post in, the copy and text, etc. is the work of a communication designer.

Making the connection to legal design

Just as important as the knowledge of service design is expertise in communication design. After all, communication and the art of making themselves and their areas of specialization understood is one of lawyers' core tasks. So why not take advantage of the wonderful opportunities offered by another profession, specifically that of a communication designer? The current developments in technology and the expectations of those seeking legal advice are now encouraging lawyers to open up to new opportunities for communicating more effectively and with greater transparency. The magic box of communication design is one of the core skills of every legal designer.

Organizational design: Organizational design is a systems and process model for establishing principles and structures for organizations to achieve specific goals. It helps to:

- Create an aligned organizational structure.
- Avoid and eliminate work silos.
- Develop the right business strategy and work out advantages over competitors so that customer satisfaction can be achieved systematically.
- Establish systems and implement workflows that drive the defined business strategy.
- Involve the right people in the relevant positions to achieve the set objectives.
- Nurture open communication and collaboration and develop an appropriate leadership style.

All organizational design activities follow the principle of increasing profitability and revenue by aligning all relevant resources with the defined goals, values and philosophies of a business or organization.

Organizational designers use the tools of design to impact and shape an organization at several levels. They have deep knowledge of design methodologies and tools, and they use these to enhance organizational culture, boost collaboration and teamwork, improve and streamline structures and processes (mainly focused on the organizational chart, structure and team functions), enable learning and development, and ultimately create an environment filled with purpose for the employees who work in it.

An organizational designer's end output, like that of a business designer, will usually be strategic recommendations for transformation and change based on the information they have gathered. This is followed by a plan of action for the implementation of those strategic recommendations. An organizational designer will then often collaborate with other designers, management and other professionals within the organization to implement the created vision and strategy.

Making the connection to legal design

Organizational design is one of the design skill sets that we are seeing increase within legal organizations. Through legal design, many organizational design principles can be translated into the legal workplace and brought into line with other industries. Methods such as "agility" and "new work" are models that lead to multidisciplinarity and a better understanding of the numerous opportunities that can also be used for legal organizations. By the way, this method of transforming legal entities should not be seen as an objective in itself, but rather as a way of improving how products and services can be designed effectively and multi-dimensionally. In addition, with the advent of the COVID-19 pandemic, many legal teams have found themselves needing to shift organization and reporting structures to those that are more decentralized and digital. Organizational design experts create the strategy to enable such change and transformation at a pace that aligns with business.

Again, the impact created by an organizational designer's strategic collaboration is generally not immediate, but rather gained over a longer period of time. A strategy is not a concrete object that people can touch, and as such, we have observed that the organizational designer's role in legal ecosystems is often overlooked or underappreciated. Many lawyers feel that they can easily be "organizational designers" after a one-week crash course in design thinking. While such self-confidence is to be admired, we must also question why this is so? Could this underappreciation of intangible design skills be a result of limited knowledge on the topic? We see organizational designers embedded in several large organizations in other industries, and we believe that going forward, law firms, too, will be embedding *real* organizational designers as key and integral personnel within their companies. These organizational designers may have degrees in both design and law, or perhaps in pure design – at a minimum, they will have some years of experience in organizational design.

Systems design and systems thinking: Systems design includes several dimensions. It is a combination of product design and systems theory. While in product design there are certain requirements regarding form, function, data and interface, the teaching of complex systems adds different aspects. These range from evolution and adaptation to existing forms of behavior in human ecosystems.

Systems thinking goes back to Peter Senge, who, in the 1990s, already laid the foundation for so-called "learning organizations."[13]

13 Senge, *The Fifth Discipline*

We do not want to go into detail here, but these two topics should be mentioned in the context of legal design. In our projects, we are always working with organizations in law firms and/or in-house legal departments that are part of a particular ecosystem. So when we cope with designing change and innovation, we find certain system patterns that we have to deal with, and many legal design projects also have an impact on those larger systems. We regularly encounter topics like "new work" and questions about how legal work must and should take place in the future. We therefore consider it important to think about such system-shaping dimensions here.

Making the connection to legal design

Generally, legal functions exist as a subset within a larger organization or context. As we seek to influence, innovate and change legal services, products and environments with legal design, we should consider the impacts such changes will have on the greater ecosystem. By adopting systems design and systems thinking, we can clearly identify positive flow effects and the impacts that changes in legal functions will have on other areas of the business.

Business design: Similarly to the way that the field of legal design is only just forming, the field of business design came into existence only a couple of decades ago. First coined by the Roger Martin at the Rotman School of Management, business design can be defined as a learning system for managers and leaders that changes how businesses innovate. It applies the methods of design thinking, in addition to other traditional business tools, to change how organizations function. To this extent, a business designer has a robust knowledge of business – including processes, business models, management, leadership and strategy – and simultaneously understands how to use design thinking (discussed more below) to shape human-centered business decision-making and practices.

Making the connection to legal design

In the context of legal design, business design is usually used concurrently with the development of any new service or product to determine a user-centric value proposition and a user-centric business development plan. It is important to consider traditional business paradigms such as: What features will entice users the most? What business model should we adopt for this new solution? How might it impact revenues? What are the channels for distribution? How can we scale this solution across markets and jurisdictions? How do we educate staff and stakeholders about these new solutions? However, for each of these questions, it is crucial to assess the business strategy with a customer-centric lens. This is essentially the business side of legal design.

Tangible design skill sets

Tangible design skill sets are usually easier for non-designers to grasp, because their contribution and value-add is immediately noticeable. Tangible design skill sets are often the skill sets most legal professionals think of when they hear the word "design." Below we list and describe some of the most common tangible design skill sets for legal design projects.

Product design is the discipline of researching, ideating, conceptualizing and building products that better fit within the lives of consumers. Effective product design balances functionality with the form and emotional benefits of the product.

Making the connection to legal design

As soon as you start making your product ideas for any legal design challenge tangible, you will need to draw upon product design principles. How do you create legal products that balance design and functionality with form and emotional benefits? Product design will help you achieve this.

User experience design (UX): A common mistake made by people who lack design knowledge is to refer to experience design (XD) as user experience design (UX). But as you will see, UX is a discrete design skill set in itself – not to be confused with XD. UX is the design of the interaction between users and products, mainly relating to digital products. The aim of UX is to make digital products or interfaces as easy and pleasant to use on electronic devices as possible. UX designers' technical abilities include wireframing, coding, app development, graphic design and interaction design. Contrasted with the invisible design skill sets, a UX designer's output can be recognized instantly, as it takes form in a tangible manner.

Making the connection to legal design

As we observe an increasing demand and need for technological solutions in the legal industry (or at least solutions that have a technological component to them), there is great need for UX in order to ensure that digital products and interfaces are designed well, easily navigable and overall create a pleasant experience. UX is relevant for all digital solutions, from web pages to apps and legal technology solutions in which users must interact with an interface on a screen.

User interface design (UI): Where UX is focused on the interaction between a user and a product, UI aims to create the best possible interface between them. An interface can be as simple as a button or as complex as a global corporation's purchasing software. UI designers always have the user's perspective in mind and their goal is to communicate any complexity as simple and understandable as possible.

Making the connection to legal design

As legal content tends to be overwhelmingly complex for most users, a good interface can help tremendously in continuous user involvement and binding them to a solution – if that solution delivers quality UI *and* UX.

Interaction design: Interaction Design (IxD) is the design of interactive products and services in which a designer's focus goes beyond the item in development to include the *way* users will interact with it. Although most people think this is only important when creating digital products, the term also applies to understanding how people interact with non-digital products.[14]

"Interaction Design is the creation of a dialogue between a person and a product, system, or service. This dialogue is both physical and emotional in nature and is manifested in the interplay between form, function, and technology as experienced over time."[15]

Interaction designers utilize all five dimensions to consider the interactions between a user and a product or service in a *holistic* way.[16]

Words (1D) encompass text, such as button labels, which help convey the right amount of information to users. Visual representations (2D) are graphic elements such as images, typography and icons that aid in user interaction. Physical objects/space (3D) involves the media through which users interact with the product or service – for instance, a laptop via a mouse or a mobile phone via fingers.[17] There is also time (4D) and behavior (5D).

IxD and UX

As mentioned above, IxD is sometimes also used as a synonym for UX. This is mainly because these two areas have a lot of overlap.

14 Kolko, *Thoughts on Interaction Design*

15 Kolko, *Thoughts on Interaction Design,* 15

16 IxD's five dimensions were first defined by Gillian Crampton Smith, a professor at London's Royal College of Art, and Kevin Silver, a senior interaction designer. This is described in the blog "Interaction Design" by the Interaction Design Foundation. https://www.interaction-design.org/literature/topics/interaction-design

17 Interaction Design Foundation, "Interaction Design"

A designer's work in IxD involves five dimensions:

I	**Words**
II	**Visual representations**
III	**Physical objects/space**
IV	**Time**
V	**Behavior**

UX involves designing the user's experience of a product, and a large part of that experience involves the necessary interaction (IxX) between the user and the product (or service). But UX goes even further, because it does not focus only on the moment of use and how to improve the interactive experience at that moment. UX is about the entire user journey, which includes other aspects such as branding, design, usability and function.
Interaction design is therefore central to the user experience, since the moment of use is the acid test of a design, where the designer's manipulation of the five dimensions must provide a satisfactory (or better than satisfactory!) experience for the users. For example, if users are hindered by unattractive features such as excessively long texts or incomprehensible animations, the design will fail regardless of the brand behind it. Interaction design is therefore one of the most important elements when it comes to the success of a product or service.

Making the connection to legal design

Interaction design is at the heart of the user experience and is a key skill that is needed for creating useful tools in the legal industry. We cannot stress enough at this point how important knowledge in this area is for legal design. Of course, this deep understanding and practical experience cannot always be united in a single person. But we can only encourage all lawyers to involve professionals such as interaction designers and UX designers in the development of new solutions. This will lead to a real boost in innovation and improved interaction between lawyers and clients.

Information architecture

Another important aspect of good interaction design is the ability to structure information in such a way that it fits the system in question – such as a website, software, intranet or similar. As part of information science, information architecture is a very important piece in the puzzle of how and where to use design, with all its categories, to master existing legal challenges in an age of change.

Making the connection to legal design

Generally, legal solutions contain words. As such, information architecture and the ability to design information – the flow, the spacing, the language used – in an easy to understand and readable manner is crucial to legal design.

Visual design, which is closely related to graphic design, is the design of media in support of visual communication. As such, it focuses on communicating information and messaging effectively through the skillful use of graphic hierarchy and visual storytelling elements such as images, colors and fonts. A successful visual design ensures that content is communicated in an engaging and effective way and is consistent with the brand of a product or organization.

Making the connection to legal design

Perhaps the most intuitive of all design skill sets for the non-designer, visual and graphic design is usually the first thought that comes to legal professionals' minds when they hear the term "legal design." Through visual depictions, illustrations and graphics, it is possible communicate complex legal information (both on paper and online) more clearly, enhancing accessibility and transparency in the law. In addition, visual and graphic design can assist legal teams in creating user-centric legal contracts that will impact overall business efficacy.

Design as a process

The way that designers solve complex problems has been given the name "design thinking." Interestingly, many designers do not feel an affinity to this term. This is understandable, as the term "design thinking" is in essence a cleverly devised term created in order to teach (and to some extent advertise) the designer's process to "non-design" professionals. We believe that the more we can instill and build designerly capabilities within "non-design" professionals, the closer we will come to creating workplaces, jobs and interactions that are both meaningful and purpose-driven. As such, even though we are designers, we are advocates of design thinking. We also take the view that the term "design thinking" makes the design process accessible to all and gives us a way of talking about the design process in an easy to understand way.

There are several definitions for design thinking, the most commonly referenced being that by Tim Brown, former CEO of the design agency IDEO. He defines design thinking as:

"A human-centered approach to innovation that draws from the designer's toolkit to integrate the needs of people, the possibilities of technology, and the requirements for business success." [18]

Design thinking provides a useful outline of the "phases" or common "milestones" a designer goes through when solving complex problems and developing new solutions. It has received widespread attention and recognition as a way to influence greater empathy, agility, experimentation and ultimately customer-directed innovation within businesses. There are

18 Brown, *IDEO Design Thinking*

several design thinking "blueprints," such as IDEO's, Hasso Plattner Institute's, Stanford University's, The Double Diamond model by the British Design Council and even Google's Design Sprint process, to name a few. While each of these design thinking blueprints may differ in its details, the essence and key steps in design thinking are common to all. Irrespective of which design thinking blueprint you use, each one starts with developing understanding or empathy, then moves on to defining the problem that needs to be solved. After this, time is spent "ideating" possible solutions, followed by extensive prototyping, testing and iterating. Finally, the idea is implemented.

The legal design process, which you will discover in Chapter 4, uses the design thinking blueprint as a backbone for innovation in the legal industry. However, it also incorporates other innovation methods, legal knowledge and business practices.

We can sum up design as multifaceted.

As you can see, "design" is extensive and multifaceted in nature. Design is a theory, a mindset, a skill set and a process. For us, it is our mission to dispel the myth that "design" relates only to visuals and aesthetics. As a legal professional reading this book, you now should have an astute foundational knowledge and understanding of legal design, and you will be able to talk about design more comfortably. It is this holistic, multifaceted definition of design that we refer to when we speak about legal design.

So what is Legal Design?

Legal design is "design deployed in the field of law to transform legal products, services, work, systems, business strategies, ecosystems and user experience."

This means deploying design in its entirety, from the human-centered mindset to each different design skill set, and using the design process (aka design thinking) in our everyday work.

We should also highlight that legal design also includes holistically leveraging legal knowledge and traditional business strategies together with design.

With this holistic and thorough understanding of what legal design really is, it becomes evident that it is a game changer for the legal industry – not only for new products and services, but particularly in terms of client-centric service transformation and systemic changes to the legal sector as whole.

Legal Design

The Law +

Experience Design, XD

Service Design

Communication Design

Organizational Design

Systems Design & Systems Thinking

Business Design

Product Design

User Experience Design, UX

User Interface Design, UI

Interaction Design, IxD

Information Architecture

Visual Design

Legal Design is Not...

- Making contracts look nice.
- Applying graphic design to legal content.
- Combining text with icons.
- Using colors instead of only black and white.
- Marketing.
- Website design.
- Interior design for law firms (although you could apply legal design to create a useful and engaging interior layout for a law firm).
- Something to learn in only a one day workshop.

- Nice to have – legal design should be in the DNA of every legal industry player (whether it is a law firm, an in-house legal department or a legal tech company).
- An ability you gain over night - it needs education and practice like building any skill.
- A title lawyers should use too quickly.
- A title designers should use too quickly.
- A fixed science – yet (but we are getting there).
- A protected professional title (yet).

Chapter 2
What is Legal Design?

Chapter 3
Why Legal Design?

3

Why Legal Design?

Chapter 3
Why Legal Design?

Now that we have established an understanding of what legal design is, it is time for us to explore more deeply *why* legal design is so important for everyone working in, practicing and interacting with legal services.

In this modern and digital age of business, the pace of evolution is fast. As a result of this rapid development, there are several new challenges that legal professionals and those interacting with legal services face on a day-to-day basis. These challenges vary from new working styles, changing client preferences, digitization and digitalization to changes in business practices, billable models, expectations and business pressures.

In this chapter, we explore these new challenges and detail why and how legal design can assist in alleviating and overcoming each of these challenges.

CHALLENGE 1

New Pressures for In-House Legal Teams

One of the most crucial drivers for innovation are huge shifts in budgets and expectations when it comes to the billing and pricing of legal services.[19] It is no secret that in-house counsel, along with other clients' of law firms and Big Four consulting groups are no longer satisfied with the billable hour system. This is the result of new billing and pricing models arising in the market and tighter purse strings affecting many organizations' willingness to spend money on external lawyers. In-house attorneys are under increased pressure from their organizations to regularly seek alternative pricing structures that deliver greater certainty, especially with respect to budget predictability. The mantra "doing ever more with ever less"[20] is the new normal and as such, it extends itself to frugality when considering legal service providers.

But budget predictability alone is not what is driving the need for change and innovation in-house. The role of the in-house lawyer has evolved into one that not only delivers legal certainty for a business, but is now also tasked with the responsibility of transforming legal business units (both digitally and otherwise) to be more than cost centers. The result is an increasing necessity and pressure to deploy new experts, methods and tools such as legal design and technology to solve the array of legal and business challenges, particularly those related to efficiency.

19 DeStefano, *Legal Upheaval*, 13

20 Cohen, "What Does 'More With Less' Mean For The Legal Industry?"

This business pressure has already led to some major changes that we will discuss in the following section. Let's take a look at these together:

Alternative service models

Up until a few years ago there were not many options to choose from when it came to legal services. But today, the landscape of providers and offerings has changed and expanded significantly. In-house legal functions have been tasked with achieving greater innovation, precision and business efficacy with smaller budgets.

The effect is that law firms are (and have been) forced to meet the new expectations and demands from their in-house clients, who are seeking more flexible payment models such as service bundles with fixed prices for certain legal services or different, more efficient approaches to working that will reduce time and ultimately, costs.

Organizations like Axiom or Lawyers on Demand (LOD) saw this need as a business opportunity to offer a different and more flexible legal service model. The two providers mentioned differ from traditional law firms. Instead of large framework agreements with a law firm, they offer a broader range of business models. Depending on the requirements of a given task, they assign lawyers with practical experience – for example, in in-house projects – to come up with a flexible solution, and in some cases to also combine it with a "fixed price model." In addition, we have seen that alternative legal services providers (ALSP) are making more and more of an impact, even in large, multimillion dollar deals usually represented by top tier law firms.

Conclusion: The expectation of more flexible legal solutions and a better cost model requires innovative ideas. Law firms have more competitors than in the past.

Cost pressure phenomenon

Despite the presence of new market players, the usual legal consultancy business has not changed dramatically yet. Furthermore, many law firms even deny the existence of cost pressure because astonishingly, their revenues are mostly still increasing.[21] One reason for this could be that clients are extremely happy with traditional legal services, but as we have already learned, most clients are not satisfied with the old pricing model. Therefore, we must attribute this increase in revenue to other factors. These include the growing complexity of our world and new developments in digital solutions, especially artificial intelligence (AI), which have all led to more and more regulations and thus, to an even higher demand and need for legal advice.

Our complex world leads to a flood of regulations. The demand for legal advice is high, but this does not automatically mean that clients are happy or even satisfied with the traditional legal business model. Additional work does not correlate to boost client satisfaction. Should a player enter the field who offers a client-centric approach combined with top legal advice, they will likely gain a large competitive advantage.

Doing more in-house

Since in-house legal departments are subject to the cost pressure described above, they are more and more concerned with the question of which tasks they can solve internally and which have to be outsourced.[22] We have even observed a massive growth in new in-house legal structures called legal operations professionals (LOPs). This has had an enormous impact on law firms. Clients are exercising increased selectivity, choosing very carefully what tasks they want to outsource to law firms. This is often accompanied by tough price negotiations and supported by procurement departments

21 Thomson Reuters, *2019 Law Firms Business Leaders Report*

22 Veith et al., *Legal Operations*

that act according to fixed purchasing guidelines. The growing number of business development departments in law firms and the established pitch culture, which is part of almost every mandate now, is proof enough of this.

The trend toward doing more legal tasks in-house is unstoppable. Law firms need to develop attractive offerings for their clients.

How could legal design address these challenges?

Given the evolution of legal structures, especially in-house, lawyers need to acquire new skills that enable them to adapt to change, keep pace with new developments and tap into their innovative potential to develop new business models and service delivery options. A study by the Boston Consulting Group and Bucerius Law School states that "if lawyers are skeptical about change and adopt a conservative stance, they may resist the idea of establishing a legal operating function."[23]

What this demonstrates is that lawyers who remain fixated on traditional models are likely to prevent much-needed change from taking place within legal environments.

It is therefore first of all an issue of attitude and mindset towards change and openness to new and flexible solutions. Special skills and knowledge are required so that new models can first be accepted and then implemented successfully.

23 Veith et al., *Legal Operations*, 18

This is where legal design as a new skill set can be of great assistance to legal professionals. The toolbox of legal design holds practical exercises and explanations on how to:

- Develop a mindset for radical collaboration.
- Identify clients' real needs.
- Co-create solutions for better legal systems and invent new cost models that suit clients' demands and wishes.

Legal design methods and processes will assist legal professionals in looking at their business from a new perspective and accordingly, responding to change with a client-centric outlook.

CHALLENGE 2

Traditional Legal Business Meets Legal Technology

In today's age of digital transformation, lawyers are confronted with expectations regarding more flexible delivery options for their services and the possibilities offered by technology.

In recent years, we have observed an enormous increase in legal tech companies offering digital service models that streamline legal business processes and reduce costs, in addition to many business services that help legal organizations (for example, to maintain and manage their contracts digitally). Interestingly, there are also many providers that offer classic legal advice via platforms and apps in a not-so-legal format. Legal advice is provided to consumers in such an easy-to-understand way that a consumer may not even realize that they have received legal advice.

Legal tech in the B2C sector

One tangible example of this type of "covert legal advice" is compensation platforms and apps for delayed flights:[24] these business-to-consumer (B2C) platforms automatically process legal questions from consumers and provide accurate advice.

How do they work? In the case of a delayed flight, a simple online question and answer technique proves within seconds whether a passenger is eligible and entitled to compensation from an airline. The backend structure of these Q&As is an algorithm fed by fixed and simple rules from the terms and conditions that follows a legal consequence logic. Within seconds, passengers are informed of their legal position and are provided with instructions outlining how to deal with it. Most of these platforms even offer the immediate payment of a certain percentage of the sum of the respective damages in return for assignment of the claim against the airline.

This example clearly demonstrates how feasible it is to provide a service for quick, efficient and simple legal solutions and legal claims. These app-based services are essentially legal services marketed in a more customer-centric way.

This demand for convenience is now also beginning to influence more complex legal matters. Lawyers are expected to deliver easy-to-access digital solutions for an array of legal problems. A positive example in the business context is the no-code provider BRYTER.[25] This legal tech vendor enables lawyers without programming skills to build simple digital applications. The principle of the "LEGO® construction kit" works particularly well for logical legal sequences and can quickly offer clients a digital solution that they can use either internally or to serve their own clients.

24 E.g., flightright.de

25 https://bryter.io/

Legal tech in courts and justice

Along with business, courts are also under a growing pressure to offer digital options and interactions in order to "...displace and revolutionize conventional working habits and bring radical change..."[26] In the drive to transform the traditional court systems and do things differently, technology plays a major role. Many initiatives are now arising across the globe, aimed specifically at tackling the technological challenges of and for courts.[27] Now in particular, with the push that has come from the COVID-19 pandemic we could (and hopefully will) see increased transformation from analogue processes to digital forms in official court matters.

How could legal design address these challenges?

What is the use of digitizing and digitalizing legal processes if they are not intuitive and user-friendly? Developing technology is the easy part. Designing it so that people will want to use it and *will* use it is the difficult part. Legal design is the perfect tool for designing legal technology that will not only provide legal certainty, but also a simple, smooth experience for the users. This is because of legal design's human-centered approach, which puts the user at the center of the action.

The legal design toolkit enables us to:

- Break complex systems down into simple structures and workflows.
- Find opportunities for standardization and automation.
- Develop new, feasible ideas for smoother, digitally-based services.
- Simplify legal content and foster access to justice.

26 Susskind, *Online Courts*, 34

27 For example, the "Denkfabrik Legal Tech," initiated by the Bavarian State Ministry of Justice. https://www.rechtsstandortbayern.de/startseite.html

Legal Transformation

When we talk about legal transformation, we have to keep in mind the right vocabulary and its specific meanings. Most of the time, there are three expressions that require a closer look and precise definitions. These are “digitization,” “digitalization” and “digital transformation.”

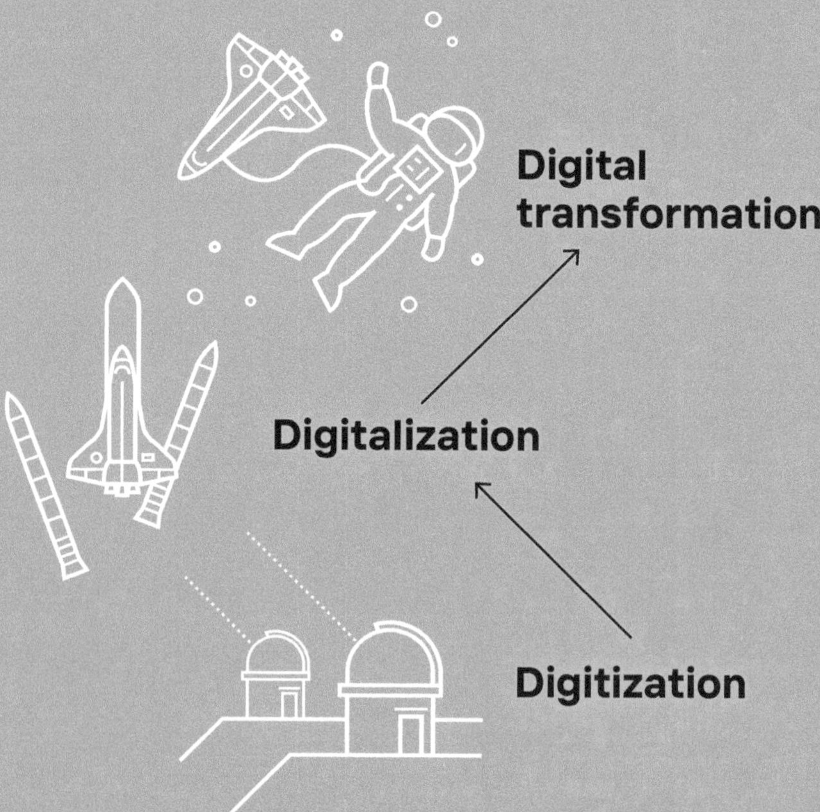

Digitization is the digital representation of what already exists. An example would be a pdf document, which is basically like a "photo" of an existing document. Pdf is the most common file type used when scanning documents to create digital versions of existing documents. Most of us scan and upload documents every day, and in doing so, we make the working environment as a whole digitally accessible. In simple terms, digitization is the process of going from analogue to digital.

Digitalization, on the other hand, means making the contents of already-digitized material more accessible. An example of this would be an AI application of a contract analysis tool. Providers such as Leverton, Kira and others are able to detect the content and its semantic relationships out of existing documents, whether they are digital representations of physical documents or digital files. So digitalization is one step further than the mere representation of a document (i.e., digitization).

Digital transformation is even more advanced and represents a radically changed way of working. "It is about using technology to allow us to perform tasks and deliver services that would not have been possible, or even conceivable, in the past."[28] Therefore, the expression "digital transformation" does not mean automation by streamlining a current system in a digital way. Instead, it means to "transform, disrupt and bring radical change."[29]

---

28 Susskind, *Online Courts*, 34

29 Susskind, *Online Courts*, 34

CHALLENGE 3

The Way We Consume Information Has Changed

Service culture – Convenience is king!

We are all consumers, and as digitalization in all areas of our lives progresses, we develop higher expectations of the way services and products are presented to us. We are enthusiastic about seamless service experiences and learn in everyday life how pleasant a smooth delivery or pickup service and enhanced convenience provided by apps such as Uber feel. We are constantly learning how pleasant and *easy* such offers are to experience – offers that meet our needs and even often anticipate our desires before we are aware of them ourselves. That same ease, convenience and experience that we so readily welcome in everyday life should extend to the area of law, too.

This much must be revealed at this point: The majority of the products and services that seem so practical to us are based on a certain development and innovation method known as "design thinking."[30] We introduced you to this framework for innovation in Chapter 2: What is Legal Design?

It's no secret, but still, people often fail to consciously stop and acknowledge that all of these nice-to-use products and services do not just fall from the sky. On the contrary: there is a lot of work and development that goes into these solutions, which focus on the user and their needs. Based on our experience and that of many others, it is clear that designing and developing something "simple" usually takes much more time and effort than designing something more complex.

30 See also the book *Change by Design* by Tim Brown

The most successful innovation method of all time, "design thinking," which is a primary backbone of legal design, offers just the right guidelines to ensure that your end solutions will resonate completely with your audience and also seamlessly fit their lifestyles.

Visuals

Technical evolution is also changing our visual expectations and the way we experience information and content. We use our mobile phones almost 24/7, and have long gotten used to consuming information in "quick snippets." Even more so, we have become accustomed to reading these "quick snippets" from our small mobile phone or personal electronic device (PED) screens. In addition, the human attention span is decreasing, a direct result of our internet era and living in the convenience economy. There are countless studies on how it is becoming increasingly more difficult for both children and adults to understand and engage with longer texts.[31] As such, infographics and intuitive user design have a more important place in today's society and have also taught us that simplified design leads to better and clearer understandability.

A simple example: emoticons, vector graphics and icons have long since found their way into everyday life – in both private and professional contexts. This is nothing else but the work of designers who have dealt with the obvious need for simple, cross-language comprehensibility. The billion-fold use of emoticons on our smartphones proves that long written communication is not meeting the demands of digital communication, which should be fast, clear and unambiguous.

Emoticons are much clearer and cause far fewer misunderstandings than written communication. This is particularly important, because in spoken

31 Interview: "'The Shallows'":
https://www.npr.org/templates/story/story.php?storyId=127370598&t=1610479712659

language we have a wide range of options to express our moods, communicate an opinion or emphasize a joke. In addition to melody and emphasis, we also use facial expressions and gestures when speaking. All this is eliminated in written communication. Emoticons help us to express ourselves clearly and without misinterpretation. Whether you like emoticons or not, it is a fact that almost all of us, in every age group, are using them, easily and intuitively.

But what if we decide to transfer this same experience to the law? Could this be possible? Absolutely, but it will take effort and a lot of legal design. Not many people want (or have the time) to read a 400-page contract, let alone read such a dense document on a mobile phone or PED. This situation is taken to extremes in terms of legibility when the contract text itself is not even responsively formatted – i.e., it does not automatically adapt to the size of our screens.

In recent times, judges are requesting for brevity in legal briefs, even requiring counsel to go back to the books and provide a brief that is concise and succinct.[32] If we live in a world where judges are no longer impressed by extensive, lengthy and verbose legal advice and information, then who is?

We could give other examples here, but in essence, our common expectation can be summarized as follows: In the future, law should also fit into our pockets.

How could legal design address these challenges?

The vision to transform legal services and products to fit a new digital era, using visuals like infographics, icons, plain language, and taking into consideration the way humans interact with digital devices and user interfaces are core topics for the application of legal design skills.

32 Olson, "Judges Push Brevity"

Legal design, as a mixture of material law and a unique skill set of several design fields, encompasses a whole range of tools in order to develop the new norm for legal information. Legal design education provides legal professionals with key knowledge about:

- How to simplify structures and content in a way that humans can understand.
- How to apply service design knowledge in order to create engaging new offerings.
- How to use graphic design and communication design in general.
- How to develop a good user experience, whether analogue or digital.
- How to apply interaction design skills in order to create the right touchpoint experience between people and tech.

CHALLENGE 4

A World of Regulations

Our world is becoming more and more regulated. These increased regulations are a major driving factor in the push to innovate and redesign the law. They include regulations relating to privacy, data and ethics (to name just a few), which force the legal profession to rethink their legal content and find ways to better ensure that people can access and understand it.

Most lawyers already have plenty to do to keep up with the many new regulations and advise their clients accordingly. However, in addition to this, there are a number of other responsibilities, tasks and obligations that new regulations such as the General Data Protection Regulation (GDPR) bring with them. The following example shows that in addition to legal expertise, there are other skills that lawyers must master in order to satisfy their legal obligations.

On January 21, 2019, the French National Data Protection Commission's (CNIL) restricted committee imposed a financial penalty of 50 million euros against the company Google LLC (in accordance with the GDPR), for lack of transparency, inadequate information and lack of valid consent regarding the personalization of ads.[33]

Why does this case matter in the context of our book and legal design? Let's take a look at Article 12 of the GDPR to answer this question:

Article 12	**WP 29 Guidance**
[Privacy notices must be in a] "concise, transparent, intelligible and easily accessible form, using clear and plain language	"Controllers cannot use long privacy policies that are difficult to understand or statements full of legal jargon"

Article 12 contains a specific obligation for lawyers to design privacy policies and data protection regulations clearly and transparently for themselves and their clients. If companies or their external lawyers do not comply with these requirements, they may face massive fines, penalties and reputational repercussions under GDPR.

In our experience both as lawyers and in working with lawyers, this is one of the best tangible reasons to understand why there might be a vital need to change the way contracts, privacy policies or terms and conditions are designed.

Lawyers are now required by law to use easy-to-understand language.

33 CNIL website: https://www.cnil.fr/en/cnils-restricted-committee-imposes-financial-penalty-50-million-euros-against-google-llc

As a result, we should be thinking about applying other communication design rules to make those policies and all legal information more accessible.

How could legal design address these challenges?
Legal design is essential in this era of increased regulation, as it provides legal professionals with a way to analyze and translate the respective laws and their effects on consumers in such a way that people without legal training can understand it.

As a direct mandate not only from a law like GDPR itself, but also as a principle of our new science: legal design stands for simplification, the removal of complexity and finally, transparency as the ultimate basic directive for fair "access to justice." This not only leads to better comprehensibility, but also helps lawyers to avoid liability and comply with their new legal obligations.

The law itself is requiring lawyers to change their ways and adopt more usable language and formats for providing legal advice. They must adhere to the new norm or face possible claims for damages. Legal design can assist legal professionals in abiding by the new legislative requirements to provide more readable, transparent and user-friendly disclosures while simultaneously ensuring legal compliance and an elevated user experience.

CHALLENGE 5

Collaboration – Meeting Client Expectations

Let's face it: the status quo of collaboration in the legal industry could be greatly improved. It is rare to see true, seamless collaboration taking place between legal professionals, other professionals (for example, IT experts and designers) and their clients.

However, it is interdisciplinary collaboration between various professionals that is key when it comes to innovation and developing better products and services for clients. Nowadays clients, too, are demanding this from their lawyers.

A simple example: what use is an idea for a new automated client service that may sound good in theory, but is technically impossible to implement? Would it not be better to bring an IT expert on board from the very beginning and learn from their experience? But collaboration does not only mean bringing together different experts; it is also about collaborating with customers and involving them in the development of new offerings.

It's about finding out what customers really need, and therefore it is crucial to integrate their views into the development process itself. Yet this service mentality is poorly developed in the legal market. It is a rare sight to see legal professionals and their clients working together to develop a solution – so rare and unusual that this type of behavior often garners publicity and write-ups in legal publications as being "trailblazing" in the legal industry.

For most industries – and from our experience working as designers in other industries – involving key stakeholders and clients in the development phase is business-as-usual, and it should be for the legal profession, too. In the future, co-creating with clients should not be something that causes law firms to receive praise and recognition for "doing things differently." We advocate that it should be the norm, and the minimum standard for creating effective and useful legal products and services. For now, however, the legal professionals who do adopt a client-centric approach and collaborate with stakeholders are leaders in modern legal working styles and deserve the recognition they receive.

How could legal design address these challenges?

Radical collaboration and working in cross-disciplinary teams is one of the basic principles of legal design. Diversity in professional expertise (along with other crucial elements of diversity, such as, but not limited to gender, race, religion) is essential to jointly co-creating new solutions. This is accompanied by the idea that the more diverse expert views that can be collected and contributed toward a solution, the better and more holistic insights we will gain. Legal design is built on an ethos of trust and knowledge sharing established between colleagues. To this extent, adopting legal design may be one way to shift the legal culture to one of true collaboration.

Lawyers are generally not trained in collaboration skills

There are a number of reasons why collaboration has not yet become part of the "DNA" in the legal world. A study carried out by the Liquid Legal Institute in 2018 showed that lawyers receive little training in aspects like working together with colleagues as well as with other professionals.[34] One of the most important reasons for this can be found in academia: law students are not taught the benefit, for example, of collectively solving a case. On the contrary, much of their legal training is aimed at achieving perfect results through individual work only. Collective success in work is not rewarded; rather the best person in their field of knowledge is considered best lawyer. Even in "collective work" contexts, individuals are taught to highlight their individual contributions and seek individual recognition within the collective. This "unique expert" behavior has worked for many decades, but it finds its limits in our extremely connected world today, riddled with increasingly complex legal challenges and problems to solve. No single legal expert alone can meet the expectations of clients and the great thirst for seamlessly-functioning solutions. This requires team effort, and legal education must start incorporating this into future lawyers' skill sets.

34 Kohlmeier and Santuber, "Is the Common Legal Platform a Wicked Problem?"

Clients want better communication, control of legal cost spending and transparency

According to a recent study by Wolters Kluwer, there is a large discrepancy between what law firms offer their clients and what those clients currently expect.[35] Many clients not only expect legal expertise but also new forms of collaboration and exchange of information and data. They want to use simple communication platforms that provide an overview of the progress of their cases, while at the same time showing full cost transparency and facilitating communication with the lawyer. But this is exactly what many law firms fail to achieve, because their internal structures are not designed to meet such expectations. The rise of "legal operations" teams is slowly starting to address this gap in service delivery; however, still at a slow pace. Law firms are often unable to meet these new client expectations for reasons such as fear of sharing too much internal knowledge about content or automating too many processes (to the extent that client briefs to the law firm may decrease) and sometimes even fear of sharing client contacts between colleagues. In project contexts, we have observed that sharing of knowledge among each other is something law firms in particular are reluctant to do. This can be attributed to the fact that knowledge is power in the legal world, and any specific knowledge that is shared may be used by competitors – or alternatively, reduce profitability.

Lawyers do not share enough knowledge with each other

A common law firm policy is often to not share client-relevant content among associates and partners, because there is an unspoken and underlying fear that a colleague might "steal" their mandate. There needs to be a proper discussion as to the root cause of such a fear. After all, should you not be able to trust the colleagues who play for the same team as you do? Or is the law firm model rigged to play attorneys against one another? While

35 Wolters Kluwer, "Future Ready Lawyer 2020," https://info.wolterskluwer.de/future-ready-lawyer-2020#

we will not seek to find the answers to this question in this book, a fear that relates to a lack of trust between colleagues does hint at systemic cultural deficiencies within high-performing legal professional environments. Legal design is one approach to slowly combatting this flaw.

This lack of widespread trust between colleagues hinders the sharing of knowledge among lawyers in the same firm. Sharing information and data is one of the crucial elements to a service-oriented company in which all relevant information should be available at any time when it is useful to satisfy clients and identify new opportunities for growth. The common practice of internal silo thinking prevents real collaboration, which leads in the end to customer dissatisfaction.

COVID-19 "lessons learned"

Data is key – user-centered infrastructures and workflows are crucial.

good tech for seamless communication and co-working is a competitive advantage.

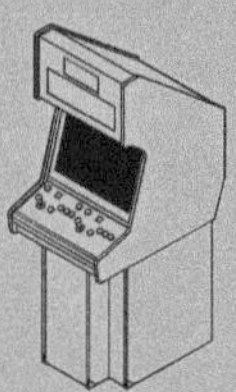

COVID-19 could be a game changer for innovation in legal organizations.

Collaboration requires training – remote collaboration even more.

Legal professionals must embrace digitalization.

CHALLENGE 6

Unique Selling Propositions

A unique selling proposition is what every company aims to achieve. It's what differentiates an organization or offering from the competition. Essential answers to the questions "What can I do better than my competitor?", "What unique knowledge and services can we offer to our clients?" and "How can we communicate that in the best way and through the right channels?" are some of the basics for good business development. But what is the outcome of such analysis in legal organizations, especially law firms?

To dive deeper, let's take a closer look at law office websites. They all more or less tell clients the same thing and use the same unique selling propositions: "We are the best in the XY practice area," "We have received X many awards," "We have completed X many high profile deals," "We have X many global offices," "Our lawyers are the most knowledgeable in their subject matter areas." Individual profiles often comprise the attorney's law school, career highlights, international experience and any possible secondments. But does this really meet the needs of potential clients? Are these really the only relevant unique selling propositions (USPs) that qualify a firm to be the "best" in law?

We can learn a lot from looking at other companies in different industries. Most companies in other industries today invest time and resources to determine their specific and unique selling propositions. What can they offer in terms of experience, products, services or culture that none of their competitors can do as well? The way they identify their strengths and key selling points is by being customer focused as opposed to competition focused. Industries such as healthcare, fast-moving consumer goods (FMCG), e-commerce giants like Amazon, and even banking see their clients and their clients' needs as the most important indicator and source of inspiration for new services and products. The legal industry instead still remains too satisfied with the strategy of promoting their own strengths, with little reference to the specific clients' needs.

A surprising experience we have had in the context of working together with law firms is the following phenomenon: many lawyers do not ask their clients what they really need. It sounds so simple, and yet it is a rare occurrence in the legal industry. Why are legal professionals averse to openly posing questions to their clients? Legal professionals often do not try to determine their clients' underlying desires when establishing their businesses – or at least they are not taught to do so. They often default to the assumption that their expertise and technical legal knowledge is enough. But that attitude will no longer be sustainable going forward.

How could legal design address these challenges?

Legal design does not only include the creative aspects of a specific challenge; it also touches on the business development and marketing aspects of the "business of law," as mentioned above.

In every legal design project, the main objective is to analyze the specific needs of the clients and stakeholders. These identified needs then serve as a basis for the development of new, innovative ideas. In other words, with our legal design approach, you get to know your customers better and learn about their weaknesses in workflows and processes. This provides a flood of information that can be used to create unique solutions. Legal design helps to change the perspective towards customer needs and to move from a push offer to a pull offer. Experience shows that this client-centric approach itself is a USP.

As shown above, far too few lawyers in law firms or in-house departments deal with the real needs of their clients (internally and externally). But how can you develop the right solutions if you do not understand what the real problems are?

As you can see, legal design is not only "nice to have"; it is, in fact, an essential basis for evolving from a traditional legal service (be it in-house or private practice) into an up-to-date or even visionary legal service provider that focuses on client centricity.

CHALLENGE 7

Innovation after 6pm only

Innovation and developing new, user-centric solutions is still not common among legal vendors. One small but crucial observation we've made from our projects is that legal teams, particularly those in a law firm context (be it a large or small law firm) actually lack many aspects innovation needs to thrive:

- There is no universal innovation strategy that is communicated and understood at all levels.
- There is little or no education or real understanding of what innovation means and the fact that it requires time, money and structure. There is a tendency to "talk about innovation," but not as much actual action. We call this "innovation theater."
- When customers ask for more flexible service models, law firms' first answer tends to jump straight to buying a legal tech solution instead of first analyzing whether a legal tech tool would be the right fit to answer and address the client's underlying problem.
- Most legal vendors/law firms talk and communicate a lot about innovation – proudly and through various channels – and yet there is little tangible evidence to demonstrate the action behind the intention. If you immerse yourself within a legal team and observe the roles each person plays (this is something our work has us doing all the time), you will see that:

- First, most innovation work is a voluntary task in addition to the workload.
- Second, the professionals undertaking innovation work tend to be young associates, junior members and professionals from business, marketing and tech.
- Third, senior figures may do the public speaking, but they are rarely rolling up their sleeves and truly contributing to the innovation process. This makes sense given the current billable hour business model. It does not make sense to deploy the most "expensive" assets into work streams that may not deliver a return on investment.

The result of this setup, however, is that those who have taken on the role of "innovators" within their legal teams must lead these initiatives in their additional time, since more often than not, such initiatives are not linked to bonus structures or significant rewards.

This leads to our so-called "innovation after 6pm" mentality: young lawyers drive new ideas in small groups without partners as an extra workload and do not get any real compensation or incentivization for it. Associates see it as an opportunity to prepare themselves for the partnership race. But this is not what innovation really is. Innovation has to be an embedded strategy in every legal business. Furthermore, it requires open minds, a collaborative environment and commitment to a real innovation strategy at all levels of the organization.

In addition to the above conundrum regarding innovation time allocation, there also needs to be room and space within legal teams to experiment, create new prototypes, embrace failure and engage from top to bottom. Innovation needs to become a part of legal organizations' DNA, and not just that of a select few individuals.

How could legal design address these challenges?

One main purpose of legal design is to create innovation and change a status quo that is not aligned with the needs of the stakeholders. Innovation requires not only time, financial and physical space resources, but above all, a clear innovation strategy. This strategy must be embedded in the company's DNA and be supported by management and decision makers. Legal design supports legal organizations in developing this DNA for innovation with the involvement of all relevant stakeholders and by providing a useful toolkit of innovation methods. Legal design therefore serves as a real change management and culture booster. In addition, it helps to find the right communication strategy that satisfies all members of an ecosystem when it comes to innovation. See Chapter 5: Field Work for a case study on how the global law firm Clifford Chance is using legal design to create its innovation strategy.

Chapter 3

Why Legal Design?

Chapter 4

The Legal Design Process

4

The Legal Design Process

STEP 1

Team and Culture Building

In this book, we are encouraging you to apply legal design in projects or in daily life. But before we start, we suggest that you first ask yourself some very practical questions, such as:

- Which team should work on a problem (e.g., a core team of internal people from your organization, or a mix of internal and external experts)?
- What composition of the team would be best for analysis, building and testing? That is, what core skills are needed to solve the given challenge?
- What will the team dynamics look like? Basically, putting together an innovation and legal design team looks easy, but its formation varies from case to case.

Depending on your specific ecosystem, these variations come naturally. What we want to highlight is that you will have to build the right team based on the specific topic you are working on; there is no "one team fits all" when it comes to legal design teams and solutions.

Most important is that the culture in the company is open to innovation processes such as legal design, and that for each project, all the necessary stakeholders needed are actively integrated into the process from the outset.

STEP 2

Research and Understand

Understanding: From problem solver to problem finder

After assembling the right team for the challenge, the next step (and arguably the most crucial one) in every legal design project is to research your target audience and build understanding. It is important to build an understanding of the people for whom you are creating solutions. These people are:

- Your users: these are the people for whom you are designing the solution. They are your "target audience." You need to stand in their shoes and understand who they are, what challenges they face and what their motivations are.
- Major stakeholders: besides your target user, who else is involved or may be impacted by this challenge? What are their goals, motivations and challenges?

By building an understanding of your users and stakeholders in the ecosystem, you can identify *why* a problem exists, get to the root cause of challenges and subsequently find inspiration to solve these problems.

Finding the right problem first

When we talk about a problem that could be solved in the context of design, it is helpful to first consider your assumption of what the problem is. In reality, most people without design backgrounds tend to define their first assumption as the precise problem for which they are trying to find a solution. They then often immediately jump into an idea-finding phase and try to develop a new solution for it.

This immediate jump can be extremely dangerous, because without investigating whether the initial assumption matches the real problem, you will end up developing the wrong solution. This wrong turn usually leads to unsuccessful products and services because it does not solve the right problem!

It is therefore crucial to find the right problem first! Later on in this chapter, we will introduce you to many techniques for making sure you are dealing with the right challenge.

Our experience shows that in an estimated 90% of all cases, the initial assumption made about a problem does not match the true underlying problem.

Empathy

There is one critical skill that every legal designer needs to learn in this Research and Understand phase, and that is an empathetic mindset. This is the ability to see a task or problem from different perspectives. You need to be able to include all kinds of opinions, needs and motivations and bring them together to form a final statement of what the real need is.

Below, we have created a list of legal design research methods that will help you identify the right problem to solve and build empathy and understanding with your users.

Legal design research methods

1. Stakeholder mapping

A stakeholder map visualizes the ecosystem in which a product or service operates from a specific perspective. Stakeholder maps help to analyze and understand who is involved in a project, and how these people, organizations and other influencing aspects are connected. A stakeholder is an individual person, a group, an organization or an aspect that has a certain interest in or relationship to a specific topic or business.

A company's stakeholders can be external (with no direct relationship to the company) or internal (with a direct relationship). Both internal and external stakeholders can have an impact on a company's actions and operations or be affected by them.

How does it work?

A stakeholder map is a visual representation of the ecosystem in which you are working, and it helps you to see all the interest groups involved at a glance. Putting together a stakeholder map helps to reveal existing formal and informal relationships between stakeholders, identify any friction between them and find new business opportunities by establishing new relationships, fostering existing ones or creating alternatives. It also helps you obtain a "big picture" overview of the ecosystem in which your problem – and thus your solution – will operate.

2. Cultural probes

This research technique was developed by Bill Gaver and his colleagues in 1999;[36] it can help you learn more about people's lives, values and thoughts. The aim is to elicit inspirational responses from people in order to understand their culture, thoughts and values better and thus stimulate the legal designer's imagination.

How does it work?

Cultural probes are empathetically designed sets of small artifacts or objects (like maps, postcards, photo cameras or diaries). These tools allow the participants to document and visualize their behaviors, habits, thoughts, feelings, interactions and wishes related to the topic of the legal innovation project within their everyday environment.

In legal design projects, for example, you can ask lawyers to document their daily work and tasks in a diary or e-journal. For instance, if you are trying to determine what legal tech tools a company may want to implement, you might ask the lawyers to document which digital tools they use, how often they use them and which ones they like and do not like. Combining this information with their documentation of feelings, frustrations and positive

36 Note: Gaver et al., "Design: Cultural Probes"

highs will give you a deep insight into the real workflows they experience in a working environment.

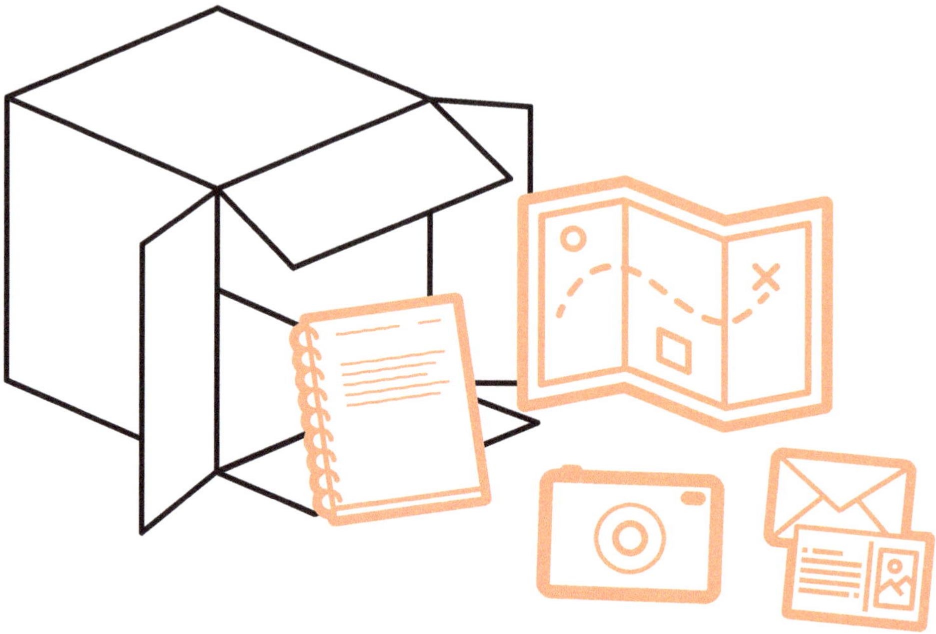

3. Persona building

Personas are fictional profiles representing specific groups of people, such as users, potential customers or employees – as well as their mindsets, needs and typical behaviors. The most important idea behind defining the characteristics of your persona(s) is to enable you to empathize with them. Try to put yourself into the shoes of someone else – such as your customer, employee, colleague, etc.

The main reason for creating personas is to get your team members aligned to a certain persona's perspective and to take that persona's specific needs and wishes into account based on the individual eco-systemic reasons that might have an influence when developing a new solution.

How does it work?

Personas illustrate the people for whom a product or service is being created. They represent your target group and allow you to understand their specific point of view in the context of the challenge you want to solve. There are several persona template sheets available, like the one we have provided below. It is important to make your personas as detailed as possible in order to bring the persona (who reflects your user) to life. Include a name, age, hobbies, a "catchy phrase" – and then dive deeper into their daily routine, challenges and goals. The team can regularly refer to the persona(s) in order to better empathize and easily understand their users' needs.

BASICS
Name
Profession
Age
Background
Interests
...

PAINPOINTS
Problems,
Barriers,
...

POWERS
Resources,
Influence
...

NEEDS
Requirements,
Essentials,
...

BEHAVIORS
Routine,
Reactions,
...

VALUES
Meaning,
Morals,
...

ASPIRATIONS
Dreams,
Role models,
...

4. Interviews

One of the best ethnographic techniques for discovering the perspectives of different stakeholders is to interview representatives of each stakeholder group. Human-centered design is about reaching the people you're designing for and hearing from them in their own words in order to learn about each person's mindset, behavior and viewpoint on a certain task in the context of the problem for which you want to find a solution. Interviewing sounds simple, but in fact it is a skill in itself. The insights obtained from an interview all depend on knowing what questions to ask. Interestingly, people often do not ask the right questions and as such do not obtain rich insights. Here is a list of basic rules you should follow when conducting interviews:

- Prepare an interview guideline.
- Prepare a setting where your interview partner feels comfortable.
- Let people introduce themselves, and show respect.
- Ask 20%, listen 80%.
- Ask permission to make an audio recording of the interview.
- Avoid biased questions.
- Avoid jumping to conclusions based on your own perspective.
- Don't ask leading questions; ask open-ended questions.
- Don't ask questions that can be answered with "yes" or "no."
- Try to find out the real reason for the problem.
- Let interview partners give you specific examples to explain their views and the reasons they think about a circumstance in a certain way.
- Don't assume a reason: ask for the real one.
- Ask relevant questions only.
- Ask always why the respective person thinks or acts in a certain way.
- Use the "5 Whys" technique: don't stop asking why until the real reason or root cause for a certain perspective emerges. Usually you will have to ask "why?" around five times.

We should point out that interviews can be held through various formats: telephone, video conference, in-person and in-person in context. Specific planning is required depending on the format. For example, have you checked whether your interviewee has the same technology as you? Can they access the video conferencing platform? How will you record the interview?

5. Observation and immersion

Putting yourself into the surroundings or "in the context" of a certain stakeholder or user helps you to explore their surroundings and see processes through their eyes.

How does it work?

In-context observation is the process of watching and detailing the movements of your users in their natural environment. For example, if you were seeking to better understand the challenges faced by everyday people appearing in court for the first time, you might set up in a court and watch the way people interact with staff, listen to the questions they ask, make note of their dispositions, notice what aspects of the court process are difficult to understand, etc.

Immersion builds on the act of observation. While observation can be likened to "sitting on the sidelines as a spectator" and taking careful notes, immersion is the act of completing the same steps, tasks and interactions as the person or persons you are observing. In other words, you are now a player in the game. Immersion allows you to not only observe but to experience for yourself and build first-hand knowledge. One example of immersion might be shadowing your boss for a day to better understand what a day in their life is like. Here, you would detail and mimic their movements, thereby gaining a deeper understanding of their routines, tasks, environment and challenges.

What sort of things should you make note of when observing? A heuristic framework that we like to adopt is the AEIOU observation framework created by Rick E. Robson:[37]

- **A**ctivities: What actions and behaviors are people taking to reach their goals?
- **E**nvironments: What is the overall setting in which the activities are taking place? How are people behaving in the environment?
- **I**nteractions: What are the basic interactions that are taking place in order for people to reach their goals? What effect do people have on activities and the environment?
- **O**bjects: What are all the details that form the environment? How do objects relate to people, activities and interactions?
- **U**sers: Who are the people being observed? What are their personalities like? How do they engage with other people in order to reach their goals?

To get the most from both observation and immersion as legal design research methods, we suggest following an observation or immersion session with a semi-structured interview with your users. This gives you the opportunity to ask why a person or people said or did a certain thing or acted in a certain way.

A	E	I	O	U
WHAT	WHERE & WHEN	HOW	WITH...	WHO

37 Note: Robson, "Building a Useful Research Tool"

6. Empathy mapping

Empathy maps assist you in delving deeper into the respective personalities and characteristics of certain target groups, including gaining an awareness of the emotional aspects.

An empathy map contains the following parts:

- Definition of the goal.
- Specific to-dos/role in the respective challenge.
- What does the user hear (from others in the ecosystem)?
- What do they do?
- What do they think and feel (divided into pains and gains):

  Pains would include questions such as "What are the person's frustrations?" "What obstacles or roadblocks are present?" "What risks may arise?"

  Gains would ask questions such as "What represents success?" "What strategies can help the person reach their goals?" "What will the person or client achieve?"
- What do they see and say?

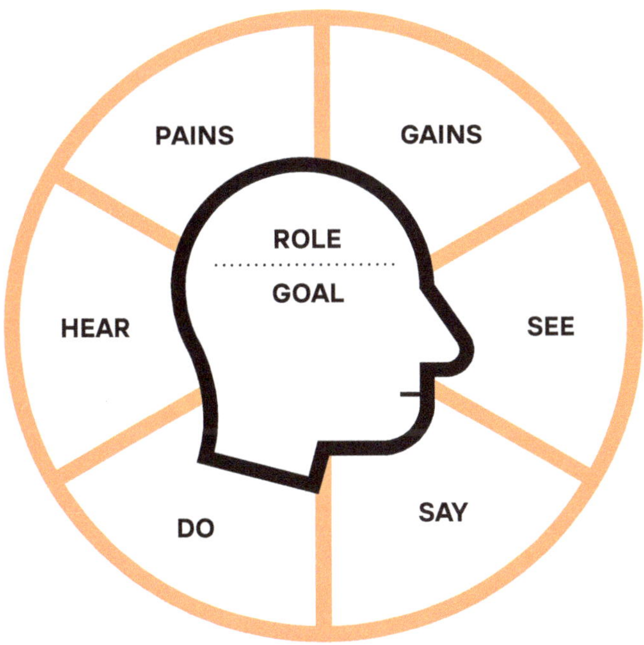

How does it work?

The best way to fill an empathy map is to ask the respective users or try to find out what a certain group of people think, feel, do and wish for. You may use a persona to help you stand in the shoes of your user when completing the empathy map.

Especially when you think about or ask for potential gains, you might get first ideas for an opportunity to build on later in the process. But understanding people, their needs and desires in the context of a certain task is crucial in every legal design project. It allows you to figure out whether your initial assumption of a problem is really the problem, or if there might be some other underlying challenges.

7. Desk research

This is a very easy and old technique: use all instruments you can to find out more about a specific problem, user or environment. Most of the time your sources will be Google and other search engines, journal articles and news articles. But let's not forget good old books and articles in magazines or other publications here. Desk research is often a good first port of call.

8. Journey mapping

Think of a journey map as a blueprint for your user. It visually represents, step by step, the experience a user goes through over time in order to achieve a certain goal.

It can be very useful to combine this technique with the so-called "jobs to be done" method. With the "jobs to be done" procedure, you analyze all the single little steps in the process a person has to go through in order to achieve a goal. The journey map requires you to plot out each milestone the user will pass in order to get there. Combined with this, you will also need to determine how the user feels at each milestone, thereby reflecting on the good and bad emotions evoked from the user's perspective in the respective situation.

Another type of journey map is called a "service blueprint" (which you can use if you are in a service environment). This also includes the different analogue and digital touchpoints on the user's journey over time and their interactions with other persons and stakeholders in an ecosystem.

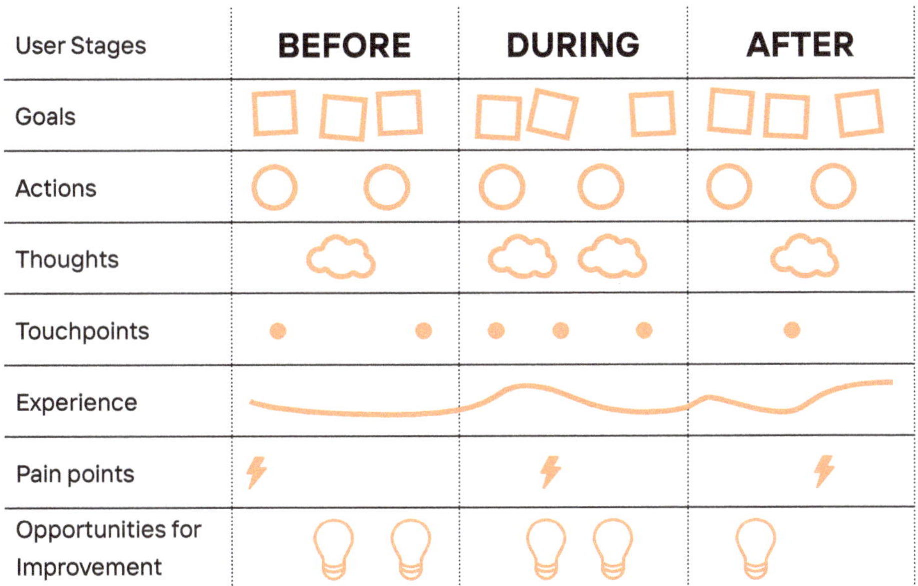

We have observed that journey maps are tools that legal professionals particularly enjoy creating and find valuable. The journey map is the best tool to choose when you want to develop or reflect on a complex workflow or when you want to analyze and improve certain aspects of a service or product. It supports you in exploring potential gaps in a system and potential solutions.

9. Surveys and polls

There is a popular opinion that taking a survey is a sufficient way to find out answers to questions and receive feedback. Surveys are still an established market research method that workplaces use. But be cautious! Receiving worthwhile feedback from surveys is not that easy!

Let's look more closely at surveys as a tool: they are very useful if you want to quickly gain a first impression of people's opinions or views on certain topics on a larger scale. So as one of the best known instruments for quantitative research, surveys can be a huge help.

But surveys and polls – especially simple ones – are tricky, since most of the time they are limited to multiple-choice answers. This means that the creator of a survey is already guiding the audience in a certain way by determining the possible answers in advance.

In many cases, an open "why" question is not part of a survey for one simple reason: it simply takes a very long time to evaluate the answers to open questions! It would also require additional effort on the part of the people taking the survey.

Many organizations decide to provide ready-made answers from which the interviewee should choose. But this is exactly what leads to fatal errors when such a survey remains the only source of research. This applies both to internal queries and to customer satisfaction surveys. Results of surveys and polls often lack deep information about specifics that could be crucial in order to find out the real needs of a user group or person.
Far too often we have seen survey results that were not worth the effort because they did not reveal any helpful background to a problem.

We are not suggesting here that you should do away with surveys entirely, but we do want to enhance your awareness of when they fit and when they can be misleading. In our experience, it is often the right choice to use surveys in addition to the other methods listed above. As a bare minimum, ensure that your surveys ask "why"-style questions.

STEP 3

Synthesize and Define

This step is about re-organizing, systemizing and prioritizing the information collected in the previous step, "Research and Understand." The goal is to uncover the exact requirements and reasons for your actual project. It is particularly important to understand contradictions and motivations, so that the "why" of a specific problem can be defined. The discovery of such gaps and the willingness to make improvements to a system are the decisive success factors in determining whether a new service or product will actually meet the identified needs later in the process.

But how can we derive insights from research?

Here are some key steps for you to follow to ensure that you draw the best insights possible from the data you have collected:

1. Data preparation and collection – get a room!

The first step is to collect all your research data at a place where you can see all the results of the work you did in the previous step in one physical space. Ideally, you should build a "research wall" in a room and literally place your research data collection on one large wall. Indeed, this is also the reason why design thinkers generally advise having a creative space in an environment where such method steps are possible. The physical room of the data collection will help you to make better connections and understand the needs of different stakeholders in an ecosystem more deeply. It is also a reason why we legal designers love sticky notes so much: they are not only a colorful way to bring your data into order; they are also a necessity during the phase of systemizing your research data and placing your results in the locations where they fit. Doing this allows you to easily identify key themes and holistically grasp your findings.

With the advent of increased remote working, particularly sparked by the COVID-19 pandemic, an alternative to a physical data room is to create a virtual whiteboard that contains all of your findings. Tools such as Mural, Miro and many others allow virtual teams to share insights in real time using their virtual whiteboard features.

Why multi-colored sticky notes and Post-Its are so handy

If you are under the impression that using Post-Its is only for aesthetic purposes to make a session look creative, please believe us that this is not correct at all! Once you have understood and experienced using sticky notes, you will understand that it is the process and act of writing or drawing, sticking Post-Its up on the wall, and the ability to easily reorganize themes and thoughts that brings much more intangible value than aesthetics. And yes, there ARE good ways and bad ways of using sticky notes. We suggest using a specific color for specific areas of thoughts, themes or opportunities. This will help you tremendously to organize and effectively collect thoughts and research data. So sticky notes are not only a nice thing to have – they are a necessary to tool for extracting critical ideas, themes, and conclusions from a flood of data in the most efficient way. Luckily, virtual whiteboards tend to feature virtual sticky notes to simulate the same experience!

2. Develop key insights

The core task when systemizing is to summarize your main findings in a concise and actionable format for communication within and across the project team. If we talk about findings, then we really mean the derivation of knowledge based on the available research data. This will lead you to the correct insights you need in order to build ideas later on in the process.

However, this also means that further research may be necessary if the existing data is not sufficient. Do not fall into the trap of "making do" with insufficient data. Not-so-experienced legal designers tend to return to their assumptions much too quickly and to use them as a basis for further considerations instead of deriving real insights. We cannot stress enough that you have to be particularly careful here. It is indeed a skill to extract the right conclusion from the existing data. The art, therefore, is to identify the situational context, the possible limitations, obstacles and frictions, and to generate the right insights.

We also want to draw your attention to something called "confirmation bias." This happens when you have already predetermined an idea or solution, and as such, you select data that supports that conclusion. Be aware of when confirmation bias may be slipping in. Remember to maintain objectivity when analyzing your data, and be prepared for findings you had not anticipated.

Why good documentation is key

If you are not sure whether you have drawn the right conclusions, check them again – and don't be afraid to do some more research. Good documentation of the data you have collected can be extremely helpful. Therefore, it is best to take films or photos for documentation purposes and to record interviews. This will enable you to look at or listen back to critical points repeatedly during the systematization phase. Now, of course, with the availability of virtual whiteboards, it is much easier to store data and analysis in the cloud.

Be mindful of privacy issues!

It is important to obtain the necessary consent from the participants in your research. Observations are confidential situations that must be treat-ed as such. Therefore, always be careful when disclosing findings and using quotations later on. Be sure that you have the appropriate consent to openly disclose the name of an organization or an individual person before doing so. Anonymized data are not a problem, of course, but again: privacy comes first! Design research requires you to take an ethical approach to collecting data and insights. Always put the needs, comforts and requests of your research participants ahead of personal gain.

3. Define the challenge by developing a point of view in a problem statement

The synthesis process described above involves the ability to puzzle together pieces of information. It is all about organizing, interpreting and making sense of the data you have gathered. This is what leads you directly to a point of view (POV) and enables you to formulate a problem statement.

The POV exercise is crucial in order to make sure that you are solving the right problem. Often, the task that you originally assumed was needed does not correspond to the actual problem to be solved.

With the POV technique, you can check the knowledge you have gained through research and compare it with the assumptions you made at the beginning of the task. This helps you to see what problem actually needs to be addressed and to formulate it using the POV technique.

In one practical case (see also the Airbus use case in Chapter 5), the task was to create non-disclosure agreements (NDAs) in such a way that they could be understood by start-up companies that didn't have their own legal departments. In the first workshop session, the assumption was made that it might be easier for start-up companies if they did not have to sign NDAs at all, and the participants discussed pursuing this idea. However, further research showed that it would have been fundamentally wrong to follow this assumption. Start-up companies very much *did* want to have NDAs in order to ensure that their intellectual property (IP) and confidential information would not be compromised. Therefore, if the participants had followed the original assumption, and the result had been to eliminate NDAs with start-ups, they would have missed the real problem. The real problem was figuring out *how* to use an NDA to create trust between a small company and a giant player in such a way that it would be possible to talk about further projects on an equal footing and to work in partnership.

There are three important components for a good POV: defining the user for whom you are writing the POV, the needs and goals you have identified through your research, and synthesizing the information you have gathered into a key takeaway. So instead of "we're eliminating NDAs with start-ups," the POV needed to be "start-up companies need a legally secure framework that generates mutual trust and allows them to share sensitive and IP-relevant information with a global player in a legally secure way."

As you can see, the formulation of the POV has to be carried out very carefully, because it defines the future framework for the solutions to the actual problem.

USER **DESCRIPTION**

Michelle, *who uses law on a daily basis,*

NEEDS **VERB**

needs *to get best possible access to law texts,*

BECAUSE **INSIGHT**

in order to be efficient.

4. HMW ("how might we..."): Finding the right question for your task

The "how might we..." question technique is very helpful in bringing together all the information and insights you have generated so far. The aim of this phase is to formulate a specific question, which is then the basis for further brainstorming. Of course, there is also a methodology for this, which will help you to find the right focus.

At first glance it may seem easy to formulate a question, but it is not quite that simple. It takes time and above all, experience, to learn how the question has to be asked so that it can be used as a basis for the next steps.

How does the HMW method work?

Now it gets tricky. The question is fed by the previous method steps. From the experience and knowledge you have gained, you need to find a question that fits the following requirements: On the one hand, it must be formulated broadly enough to avoid any creative restrictions. On the other hand, the question must be so concrete that the actual problem can also be solved in a meaningful and useful way.

The ideal HMW question can be created using the following guideline:

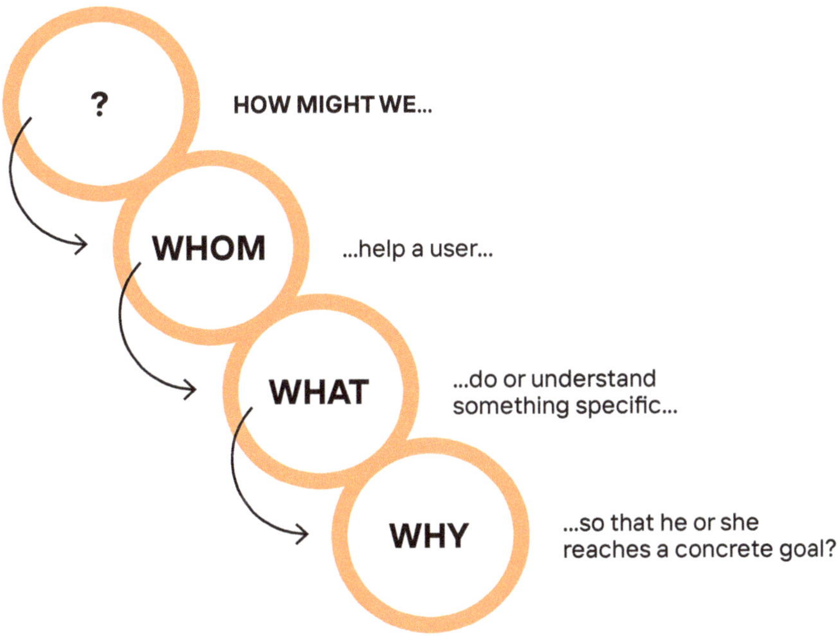

Putting it into context: for example, you may have identified that the marketing team does not understand their compliance obligations. Using the HMW method, the problem statement that you will then try to solve could be something like this:

"How might we help the marketing team understand their compliance obligations in a way that is easy to remember?"

STEP 4

Idea Development/ Conception

Once you have derived your HMW statement and thus defined the challenge that you will tackle, it is time to create solutions.

The term "ideation" is one that is not particularly accepted or liked by legal professionals. Based on our extensive field work, we have found that the word "ideate" does not resonate with them, thereby contributing to increased friction in the acceptance of design as a process within a global legal team. If we are to take a truly user-centric approach to educating legal professionals about design, then we must tailor the design vocabulary to explain design concepts in a way that makes sense for the legal mind.

To our design contemporaries reading this book, we acknowledge that changing design terminology to accommodate the preferences of legal professionals can be likened to requiring Darwin to change the way he expresses his theory of evolution to suit the vernacular preferences of lawyers. Nevertheless, lawyers are a unique bunch who are, as research proves, trained to be highly skeptical and less trusting than the general public.[38] Since our primary goal is to enhance legal design knowledge and understanding, we will do whatever it takes to ensure that professionals reading this book understand each step in the legal design process. Therefore, for the purposes of this chapter, we will forego the word "ideate" and instead use the overarching term "idea development," which comprises "idea generation" and "idea selection."

38 Richard, "The Lawyer Personality"

- Idea generation can be expressed as *creating choices*.
- Idea selection can be expressed as *making choices*.

Creative thinking – Divergent and convergent

In order to create good ideas, you need to think creatively in the first place. Creative thinking is a natural capacity of all human beings, which we explored in Chapter 1: Philosophies. Even though we are all capable of finding new ways of thinking and developing new ideas, there are some supporting methods that are easy to follow and which can help us on our creative journey.

One basic principle is the separation of "divergent" and "convergent" thinking. "Like heartbeats and breathing, creative thinking has a natural and unconscious rhythm of its own. It expands and contracts: we instinctively open up the possibilities before we narrow our choices."[39]
While divergent thinking is about opening yourself up to all thinkable and unthinkable combinations, wild imaginations and finding a creative flow that does not limit your fantasy, convergent thinking is quite the opposite. In the phase of convergent thinking, you will once again use your systems of logic and narrow down your options. But this can also be tricky. The art of convergent thinking is to not to get rid of all the wild ideas you had before, but to narrow them down while at the same time maintaining ideas that have a sufficient element of novelty or innovative quality.

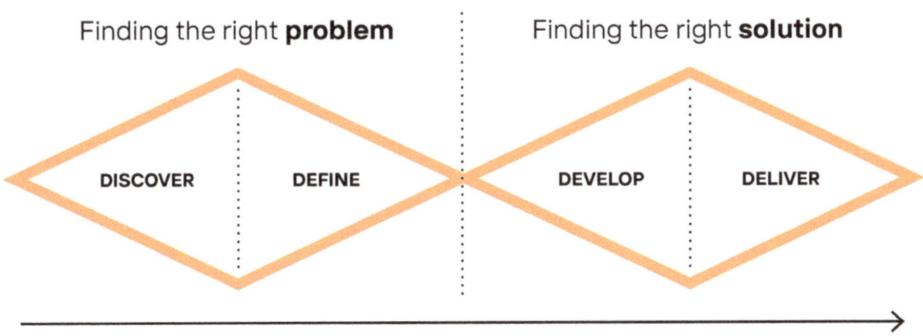

39 Nielsen and Thurber, *The Secret of the Highly Creative Thinker*, 65

The graphic on the previous page is a good representation of divergent and convergent thinking in practice. You will note that in this step of idea development, you will use both divergent and convergent thinking to complete different tasks.

Note: Divergent thinking is not about determining the feasibility of an idea!

Idea generation

Lawyers are conditioned to seek the expected "right" answers, which is definitely necessary when it comes to providing quality legal advice. This is convergent thinking: using facts to go straight to a solution. But convergent thinking doesn't generate any new ideas; nor does it inspire people to do so – something that is essential for any organization that seeks to have a truly innovative culture and develop innovative solutions.

Idea generation is a phase in which you must commit to embracing divergent thinking. Divergent thinking is the process of generating many ideas about a topic. At the idea generation phase, it is important to not focus on feasibility. Instead, you should encourage people to embrace an environment of experimentation and think up wild ideas, opening up their imaginations and thinking about what possibilities exist. Do not worry about budget, time, feasibility or any other limiting factors or constraints during this phase. You will take care of this during the "idea selection" phase.

Idea selection

The second half of the idea development process involves selecting concepts from the many ideas generated. Concept selection is an intentional way to narrow down your choices, yet preserve potential.[40] For this phase, you need to move back to convergent thinking. In order to shortlist your ideas, you should now establish a list of objective criteria by which to assess the potential feasibility of each idea. By doing this, you will ensure that your team

40 Both and Roumani, *Ideation/Creation Expedition*

is aligned on the design vision and the defined requirements the ideas should satisfy in order to progress to the prototyping phase. Some common objective criteria are:

- Costs – can the idea be launched within an established budget?
- Time – how fast do you want to launch a solution?
- Capabilities – do you have internal capabilities to realize this idea? Or do you need external assistance? If external assistance is required, do you have the budget?
- Technological feasibility – does your business currently have the technological capability to create this idea? Does the technology currently exist somewhere in the market?

Legal design rules to live by

Before starting an idea development session, it is important that you and all the other participants are in the right frame of mind. Below are seven fundamental rules every person should abide by when developing ideas:

1. Defer judgement – of others and of yourself: Most legal professionals have very high expectations of themselves and others. Such expectations may be good when writing a legal contract, but they can actually stifle your creativity when the task is to generate ideas. It is important when developing ideas to defer any judgement or critique you might feel towards any ideas at this stage. Here are two tricks we recommend whenever you feel a negative comment or critique slipping into your mind:

- Acknowledge the critique internally and then let it go. Idea development is about creating lots of ideas, not shortlisting and critiquing.
- If step one fails, ask your colleagues probing questions like "How would this work in context?", "Can you explain the idea a little further to me, please?" Do not give your opinion on the idea at this stage, but listen and learn more. During the idea selection phase (detailed above), you will have full freedom as a team to narrow down and shortlist ideas based on their pros and cons.

2. Build on colleagues' ideas: Find ways to enhance and further develop your colleagues' ideas.

3. Open environment: When we talk about an "open environment," we are referring to creating a psychologically safe environment as detailed in Chapter 1: Philosophies. Be mindful of creating an environment in which you are open to sharing your ideas, open to receiving other people's ideas and open to assessing ideas collectively and constructively.

4. Quantity over feasibility: Based on our experience, this is also a rule that is especially important to highlight for those working in law. Legal professionals are trained to "nitpick," and as result, we observe that legal teams tend to discard several ideas before giving them the time to flourish. During the idea development process, feasibility *does not matter.* Your ideas can range from simple to extremely wild and complex. The point of idea development is to generate as many ideas as possible and see how far you can push your thinking as a team to come up with a revolutionary idea.

5. Stay focused: During idea development, there is the tendency to veer off track as ideas start to grow and excitement builds. We suggest that you delegate one person the responsibility of ensuring that the team remains focused on the legal design challenge they are trying to solve. Any new ideas or thoughts relating to other matters can be quickly jotted down, and then the focus should go back to the main challenge.

6. All ideas are welcome: We want to reinforce the fact that in the idea development process, *there is no such thing as a silly idea.* Interestingly, we have found that it is often the seemingly "silly" ideas which, when shared, spark someone else's great idea. When you share your idea, whatever it may be, it immediately acts as a catalyst for other people's ideas. By holding your tongue and keeping your ideas to yourself for fear of embarrassment, you are doing yourself, your team and your organization a disservice. You should establish a sufficient level of trust among your team members to ensure that everyone shares their ideas.

7. Enjoy the process: Above all, enjoy the process. Embrace any discomfort; laugh and learn from your teammates – and rediscover your creative competencies.

Methods for idea development

There are several research-based creative methods that teams can use to generate ideas for their legal design challenges. These design methods will help you use your time effectively and efficiently, as they provide frameworks and structures for positive idea development sessions. Below is a list of methods we like to use with our clients. For most of these methods, it is important to have a facilitator running the session in order to ensure that participants are able to immerse themselves fully in the experience of collaborating and developing ideas together. This facilitator may be an external expert or someone delegated internally.

1. Brainstorming

Most people are familiar with brainstorming as a method of generating ideas. It is only one of several methods for idea development, but does achieve great results when conducted properly and with a facilitator. Group brainstorming is most successful when there is a facilitator with a large group of people. There are two styles of brainstorming: all together or individually.

What you need:

A designated facilitator (if group brainstorming), Whiteboard/flip chart, Markers/pens

Steps:

A. Describe the problem you're targeting and write it on the whiteboard or flip chart. Be sure that everyone understands it.

B. All together:

a. This is usually done in a multidisciplinary team. Team members call out their ideas, and the facilitator or scribe documents them on the whiteboard or flip chart. The facilitator should ideally be someone who can write quickly and legibly to keep up with the flurry of ideas being called out.

b. Another option in group brainstorming is to have everyone write their ideas on Post-It notes and then stick them up on the whiteboard or flip chart. The facilitator will then read out each idea and cluster together ideas that are similar to each other. This helps to organize the ideas into themes.

c. During brainstorming, the facilitator should ensure that idea development rules are being followed in order to enhance the overall experience and outcomes of the session.

C. Individually:

a. In some teams, it can be better to divide the brainstorming session into two distinct phases: idea generation and idea collection. This method of brainstorming is particularly suited for teams where there may be a strong hierarchy or several dominant voices that smother out the rest.

b. First, the teammates agree to separate and think of ideas/solutions to the problem they are targeting individually. They will document these ideas and solutions on Post-It notes. Each teammate can go wherever they find inspiration. Give people 20–30 minutes for this individual phase.

c. After the allocated time is up, the team comes back together. The facilitator will then collect each member's Post-It notes and go through them one by one, sharing them aloud with the team.

2. Round robin

This is an adaptation of the 6-3-5 method, a research-backed, group-structured brainstorming technique developed by Bernd Rohrbach in 1968.[41] Round robin is a great way to generate lots of ideas and build on each other's ideas. The purpose of round robin is to enable idea generation in a way that empowers both introverted and extroverted personalities. We've observed that this method is particularly suited to environments with legal professionals where there are often dominant voices that easily overpower others.

What you need:

Pens, Post-Its, Stopwatch/timer, Groups of 3–4 people

Steps:

A. Individually: Set the timer for 5 minutes. During these 5 minutes, each person individually sketches or writes at least three solutions to the identified problem on a standard sheet of paper. It is best to write one idea per sheet of paper.

B. Rotate: When the 5 minutes are up, hand your sheets of paper to the person on your left (clockwise). Do not provide any explanations to the person receiving your papers. For the next 3 minutes, each person builds on their teammates' ideas by adding to the papers they have received.

C. Repeat: Repeat Steps 1 and 2 until your original sheets of paper come back to you.

D. Result: A variety of ideas and possible solutions to your challenge, which have been built upon by the team.

41 "Brainwriting: Enabling Everyone to Share Their Creative Ideas," Mind Tools (website), https://www.mindtools.com/pages/article/newct_86.htm

3. Co-creation sessions

The people for whom you are designing can help a lot. Legal professionals are taught to be "solution providers" and as such, involving clients is not an intuitive practice for them. However, lawyers as a profession are doing themselves a great disservice by not being more open and collaborative with their clients.

Through the legal design process, you will talk to a lot of different stakeholders and learn many insights along the way. A co-creation session is the ideal way to keep these stakeholders involved in the process and receive real feedback from them on your current ideas and directions.
A co-creation session goes further than a general feedback session. The purpose of a co-creation session is to invite the people for whom you are designing to be involved in the design process with you. *Together* you will devise a new solution for your legal design challenge. Co-creation sessions are not just platforms for receiving feedback, but a way to empower your users to be a part of the design journey and join your team. Together, for example, you could co-create a new compliance training process, the law firm pitch deck, or a playbook on certain legal procedures. The other positive aspect of co-creation is increased buy-in and support for the solution that is generated. It goes without saying that people generally support ideas that they have been a part of generating. In our experience, solutions born from co-creation often have higher success rates in terms of adoption as well.

Steps:

A. Identify the participants and invite them to participate.

B. Determine the space for the workshop and materials required.

C. Formulate the co-creation session.

D. Host the co-creation session.

E. Capture the feedback.

F. Follow up.

Concept selection methods

You now have generated numerous possible ideas and solutions for your legal design challenge. The next step is to select the best ideas to put forward for further development. How does the team decide? In concept selection, factors such as feasibility, resource allocation, timing, originality and budget constraints need to be taken into consideration. The methods listed below will help you and your team shortlist the ideas that best suit your business needs and business constraints, while still keeping the end goal in mind and not foregoing originality.

1. How/Now/Wow (Ciao!)

The How/Now/Wow (Ciao!)[42] matrix is a fun and intuitive way to sort through the ideas you have generated.

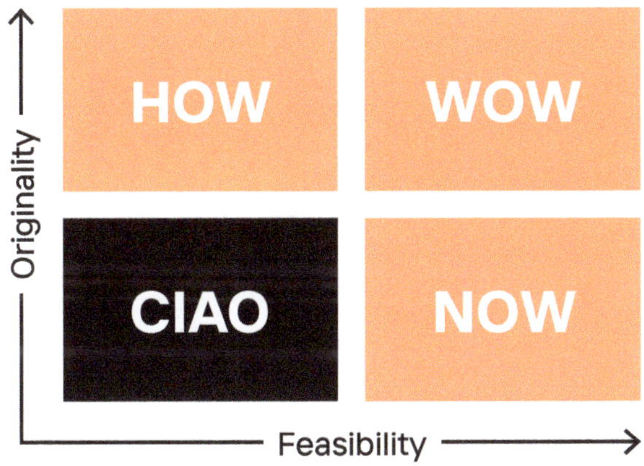

The matrix:

How: This quadrant represents ideas that are innovative, but not feasible. This area is good for setting future goals.

Now: This quadrant represents ideas that we know work well now, are easy to implement, but perhaps then are not innovative.

Wow: This quadrant designates creative ideas that can be implemented.

Ciao!: These are ideas that the team is happy to dispose of.

42 Hagen, "How|Now|Wow (Ciao!)"

What you need:

Whiteboard, Markers, Ideas generated on Post-It note

Steps:

A. Draw up the 2 x 2 matrix (pictured below) on the whiteboard.

B. Set objective criteria to consider when assessing each idea. For example, a budget of 10,000 euros or less, or implementation time.

C. As a team, talk through each idea and place it on the matrix where you feel it is appropriate.

D. Ideally, we are looking for ideas that fit into the "Wow" category.

2. Democratic vote

A speedy way to shortlist ideas to develop and build on further in the prototyping stage is through a democratic vote. However, this is not a vote conducted by show of hands.

What you need:

Stickers, Your ideas from the idea development phase written on Post-It notes (either physically on virtual sticky notes if you are using a collaborative virtual whiteboard tool)

Steps:

A. Ask each person to talk through the ideas they generated in the idea development sessions with the group. Make sure to listen to everyone's ideas and ask clarifying questions to help you understand each idea.

B. Give each person three stickers. One sticker = one vote.

C. Ask each person to cast their vote by placing stickers on or next to the idea(s) they would like to see move forward to prototyping.

D. Shortlist the ideas that received the most votes. Discuss together which ideas should proceed to prototyping.

STEP 5

Prototyping and Testing

Shifting from the abstract to the physical is a fundamental process by which we can open our minds to new possibilities[43] and assess the validity of our ideas from both an experiential and a business model perspective. Prototyping is the tool you can use to achieve this.

Out of the six phases in the legal design process, we have observed that prototyping is by far the one that legal professionals find most uncomfortable – or perhaps the least intuitive. One reason for this stems from legal education itself, which, as we explained in Chapter 1, does not include building to learn or building to think in its syllabus. The psychological aspects of prototyping have also been found to cause a certain level of discomfort among legal professionals, who are not accustomed to sharing "half-formed" ideas. It is simply not normal within legal culture to share work with third parties unless it is finalized – and yet this is exactly what prototyping demands from the legal professional: to share early-stage prototypes not only within their team, but also with a broader spectrum of stakeholders and clients. It can feel daunting.

We have seen that many legal professionals initially feel reluctant to share and test prototypes with external stakeholders for fear that it would reflect badly on their organization and their personal credibility. This apprehension, while understandable, is merely a limiting belief that legal professionals impose on themselves. The concept of prototyping, testing (for example beta testing) and iterating is common practice for most other professionals – in marketing, business strategy and technology, to name a few. We have observed that prototyping serves as a useful tool to help legal professionals

43 Brown, *Change by Design*, 87

connect with other professionals and build not only better products, but stronger relationships.

Prototype vs. MVP

We would like to stress here that the initial goal of prototyping is not to create a minimum viable product (MVP). For those wondering what an MVP is, think of an MVP as a "working draft" – a version of a product or service with just enough features to satisfy clients for early testing and feedback. A first prototype is a "rough draft" of your MVP. First prototypes are simply a tangible expression of your idea. You will create many prototypes before

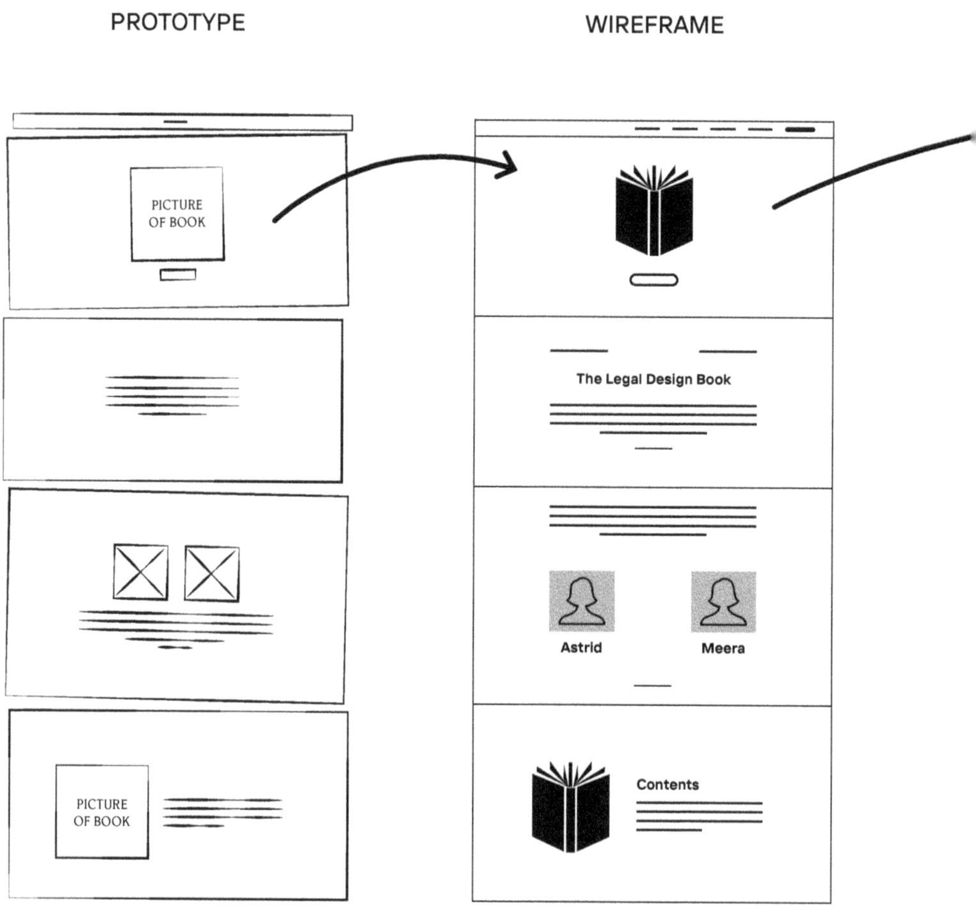

you create an MVP. Prototyping is so essential because without tangibility or giving form to an idea, it is far more difficult to assess and learn about the strengths and weaknesses of an idea or proposed solution.

A prototype allows your target audience to imagine what an experience or product would be like and how it might fit into their everyday life. Prototyping also helps teams discover and identify new directions for further development of a more refined prototype.

MVP

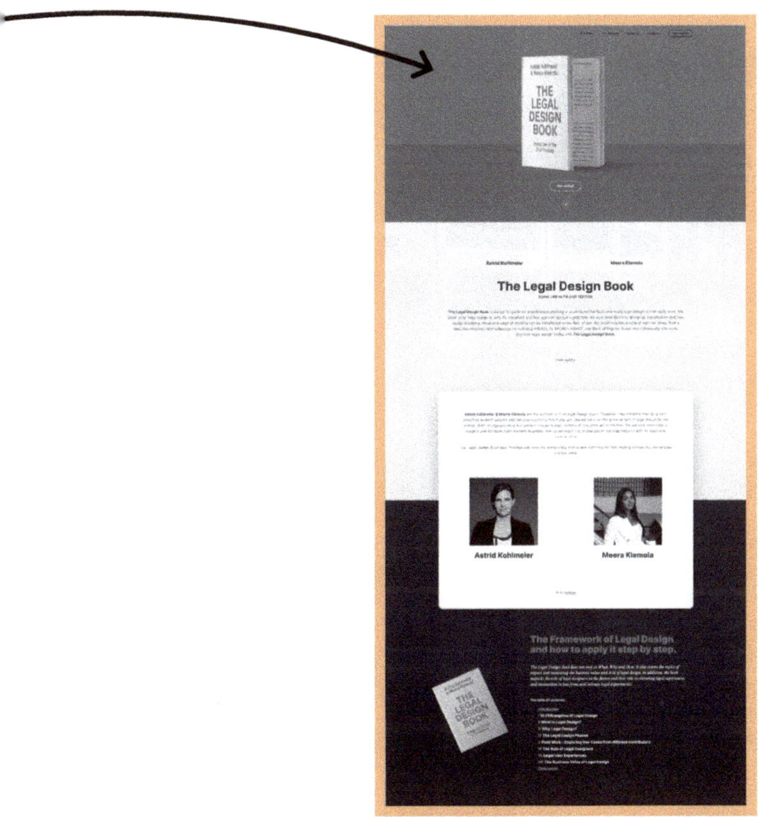

1. Prototypes

How to start

Testing goes hand in hand with the concept of prototyping. What is the use of giving form to ideas if you do not receive feedback on them? We build a prototype in order to test the prototype, to build further on the prototype, to further test the prototype, to further build the prototype... the cycle continues until we make a judgement call that the prototype is at a stage where it can be launched as a minimum viable product or service (MVP/MVS). Once the MVP/MVS is launched, testing and further development continues.

You can see the concept of building and testing is a continuous process that should continue further even as the product or service lives and breathes. This is the way to enable the evolution of products, services and experiences to ensure that you continuously deliver the best results that match or perhaps even exceed the expectations of your audience.

How to create quick prototypes

Sketch/pen and paper

The power of pen and paper should never be underestimated. What might take us 10 minutes to explain verbally can be communicated in a matter of seconds with a quick visual representation of our ideas. Sketching is a wonderful way to quickly bring tangibility to an idea and create a prototype to receive feedback.

What you need:

Pens/pencils, Paper

Steps:

A. Create a visual representation of your idea. Remember, you do not need to be Picasso in order to sketch! Simply sketch your idea conceptually in order to communicate it to others.

B. Voila! You've created a rapid prototype.

C. Now go and show your prototype to others for feedback. Talk them through the concept and ask for feedback.

2. Empathic experience

Empathic experience is a way in which a team can prototype and test the product or service in question under exaggerated limited conditions such as limited sight, hearing or dexterity. It is a great way to prototype and test an idea when the aim is to create truly inclusive products and services and to ensure that a wide range of users can use the product or service as intended. This can be a great method to use if you and your workplace have identified workplace diversity, inclusivity and accessibility to be primary characteristics for your end product or service. We have observed this to be an insightful method for people to really build empathy and understanding for the way in which users might interact and experience the product or service. It is one of our favorite methods for designing better experiences in a legal setting.

What you need:

Props, Pens, Paper, Anything you need to simulate extreme conditions.

For example, when simulating services for the elderly, you may want to use out-of-focus glasses or put Vaseline on a pair of glasses to simulate limited sight. Or you can wear ear plugs to simulate hearing loss.

Steps:

A. Define the legal design problem (e.g., design a contract automation tool that non-legal professionals can use).

B. Define typical empathic users and usage environments (marketers, business and sales professionals: they may use the tech on their phones).

C. Design empathic experiences:

Create conditions that mimic extremes (e.g., difficulty reading, hearing loss, non-verbal communication).

D. Simulate an empathic experience and test your product or service with the extreme constraints:

Limited sight – blindfold

Limited hearing – noise-cancelling headphones

Limited time – stop watch and timer

Limited dexterity

E. Synthesize findings:

What worked and why?

What did you learn?

How can you iterate the prototype to fix any problems?

Should the prototype be changed completely?

3. Wireframes

Think of a wireframe as a storyboard made specifically for user interfaces, such as computers or mobile device screens. You can see examples of typical mobile device and computer screen wireframes below. A wireframe is essentially a two-dimensional illustration of a page's interface, which focuses primarily on functions available, prioritization of content, space allocation and user behavior. A wireframe mimics the screen that users will interact with for an online product or service. It is therefore an ideal (and cheap) way to prototype and test online products and services with users before actual development takes place.

Wireframes are used early in the prototyping and development process to ascertain the basic layout and structure of a page and the way in which a user will likely interact with the page. For this reason, wireframes usually do not include graphics, colors or styling.

What you need:

User journeys, Paper, Pens, Wireframe printouts

Steps:

A. Each wireframe represents one web/app page.

B. Complete wireframes to mimic the intended website or app.

C. Test with users, observing their behavior. Is any information missing?

D. Was there any aspect that was not intuitive? What could flow better?

E. Iterate your wireframes to incorporate the feedback you receive.

4. Role-playing

When prototyping services, role-playing is a method you can use to easily test and evaluate your offering. While role-play might seem uncomfortable, one study observed that legal professionals in more senior positions actually preferred role-playing over sketching. The reason for this is that senior legal professionals are used to performing and orating: as such, role-playing is more intuitive and natural to them.

What you need:

People

Steps:

A. Identify the customer journey.

B. Assign a member of your team to take notes and observe the service in action.

C. Act out the customer journey with your team.

D. Debrief and summarize what you learned.

Tip: To make the service more concrete, include props and carry out the service in context.

STEP 6

Implementation

In this last phase of the legal design process, it is time to implement the solution. As explained by leading design thinker Tim Brown, implementation is about "communicating an idea with sufficient clarity to gain acceptance across the organization, proving it and showing that it will work in its intended market."[44] Based on our experience, the implementation phase can feel quite daunting to legal professionals, because launching a product or service and the unpredictability of the implementation phase is not something they are used to.

Implementation can be messy, and it does necessitate the ability to think on your feet and respond quickly to unexpected issues that may arise. But do not be too daunted: instead, accept the fact that it might not be smooth and let yourself experience the excitement that comes with bringing a new solution to the market brings. Below are a few of our tips for successful implementation:

Piloting: Piloting a solution, or creating a "soft" launch is a good and gentle way to begin implementation. Rather than "going live" to all possible users from the outset, select a couple of users of your solution and ask whether you can do some initial pilot testing with them. This not only eases the pressure should there be unexpected glitches, but it also allows you to test the solution "in context" over a dedicated period of time. This process works as a collaboration between you and your client, and the feedback that you receive will only help to finesse the solution for a large-scale launch. In an in-house context, piloting would take the form of arranging for one team,

44 Brown, *Change by Design*, 107

say Sales, to test the new solution and then rolling it out organization-wide over time.

Write detailed instructions: Detailed instructions are essential, particularly if your solution is a new template or product. Develop an instruction manual that users can refer to for full instructions on how to use the solution. For example, if your solution is a redesigned contract, then create a "precedent or drafting note" detailing how people should complete the relevant fields in order to prepare the redesigned contract properly.

Treat implementation as an iterative process: If you have ever been involved in tech development, you will understand that implementation and launch is not the end, but rather the beginning of continuous development. A tech solution needs to be tweaked every day; bugs need to be fixed and the solution updated. Later on down the line, new versions will be created with new features, continually adding to the overall experience. This view to continuously updating and iterating is the approach that should be taken for all legal design solutions, whether they are tech-based or not. At a minimum, set an annual review of the solution to identify what has been working well, what could be improved, whether any new features are required, whether any features are now obsolete and whether the solution can be integrated with other aspects of the business. By regularly reviewing the solution, you will be able to keep up the innovative pace and further build on the experience delivered.

Create a story to share: Do not underestimate the power of storytelling. Share your journey to date: how the team thought of the solution and created the solution; the updates and pivots that were made to get to this first version of the solution ready for implementation. Communicating the rationale and reason for the solution helps to bring more people onboard the journey and thus generates greater support for the solution. More buy-in leads to greater adoption of the solution, which is the end goal.

Legal Design research ethics

You will rely on your colleagues, stakeholders and clients to test your prototypes and provide feedback. Throughout this process, it is important to collaborate in a way that is built on trust and transparency. We would like to highlight some key legal design research ethics practices to uphold:

- Always seek permission.
- Maintain a 1:2 maximum ratio: No more than two people should interview a person at one time. You want to create an environment in which people feel comfortable and at ease. We have found that too many interviewers can leave people feeling interrogated and anxious.
- Be prepared: Respect the time that your users and stakeholders take from their day to participate in your research. Be prepared with your tasks and questions. Do not run overtime.
- Be transparent with your findings: report your findings honestly and communicate them in a respectful manner.
- Respect people's wishes.
- Protect raw data: During research and testing you will obtain a large amount of raw data. Be sure to guard people's privacy by preserving their anonymity (if requested) and storing raw data securely.
- Archive responsibly: When you no longer require your research findings and observations, be sure to store or dispose of them securely. Remember that a lot of information you collect is personal and at times, highly confidential.

Chapter 4

The Legal Design Process

Chapter 5
Field Work

5

Field Work

Chapter 5
Field Work

What does legal design look like in practice? Who is using legal design?

It's time to get practical. In this chapter, we have curated a selection of legal design projects from our clients', collaborators and other leaders in the field. The case studies included span industries and geographies, to highlight the growing global influence and impact legal design has on all legal ecosystems – be it a university, an international law firm or an internal legal department of a billion dollar company. We thank the project leaders and all contributors for sharing their great work in this book.

In addition to the six use cases, we added a list of other legal design projects online. You can find the details at the very end of this chapter. New examples of legal design projects are emerging every day, the results of which are shared regularly on social media. We encourage you, the readers, to develop an open eye for it. Use these case studies as evidence to initiate the legal design dialogue within your organization and to demonstrate to key decision makers what other players (be it competitors or otherwise) are already implementing legal design today. Such a stimulus can be the key driver to get started with a project and thus set the first legal design milestone for your team and organization.

Case studies by

Clifford Chance/
Hive Legal/
Queen Mary University/
Airbus/
Háptica/
Visual Contracts/

Clifford Chance's Innovation and Best Delivery Hub in Germany

by

Dr. Sandra Thiel,

Partner and Head of Innovation, Clifford Chance Germany

Eva Säljemar,

Continuous Improvement Project Manager, Clifford Chance Germany

1. Innovation at Clifford Chance

Innovation and legal technology have become an integral part of the legal services industry and of legal practice itself. New ways to work and collaborate offer the potential to deliver legal advice more efficiently and better adapted to clients' needs.

2. The challenge

In today's market it is not enough, even for top-ranked law firms, to simply provide legal advice of the highest standard. Such legal advice needs to be consistent with the respective client's business and operative needs. Our conclusion was that not just legal advice, but also the way it is provided, must be continuously challenged and improved. The importance of such an integrated approach increases year by year. For our own innovation and best delivery project, this means that our capacities and know-how as well as our product range all need to grow and be continuously developed. As for our established legal services, our ancillary best delivery offerings need to be continuously challenged, revised and redesigned. New products need to be developed, new approaches need to be pursued.

Our dedicated innovation and best delivery team is therefore constantly at the forefront of legal issues, technical innovation and processes. We consistently work to improve our offerings not only to clients but also internally to our firm's partners, counsels, associates and transaction lawyers ("legal professionals"). The products and processes vary from matter to matter, from sector to sector, from client to client and from issue to issue. In each case, the challenge for the Hub team was and continues to be to fully understand the particular requirements and to provide what is best for the respective matter.

We recognized the importance of fostering cross-practice, cross-office and cross-border collaboration between legal professionals and the Hub team in order to put our innovative capabilities to the best use, and we are constantly looking for techniques to help us achieve this.

Firstly, we wanted to create an integrated open space for innovation and collaboration as part of our office, where clients, legal professionals, the respective matter teams, legal project managers, best delivery teams as well as other business professionals can come together to brainstorm ideas, consider possible solutions and products and, more generally, give innovation room to grow. This was to be a physical space, bearing in mind that it was not just about providing a fancy room where you could sit on beanbags and sip soft drinks while otherwise continuing to go about your business as usual, but it should also foster a creative, agile mindset and openness for innovation.

Secondly, we wanted to ensure that the room fosters the creation of a mindset for interdisciplinary work and innovation and that we focus on the right matters. While we were literally tearing down walls in order to create what would soon become our collaboration space, we decided to get Astrid on board to refine and sharpen our approach and to ensure that we were also targeting the right issues and changing the mindset of our people; in other words: to create a user-centric physical and virtual space for innovation and implementation – our "Innovation and Best Delivery Hub" or simply "Hub."

The aim of our initial legal design project was to define a purpose and customer-oriented vision statement and working concept for the Hub while taking into account the global firm strategy and local market demands. On that basis, we asked ourselves:

How can the Hub help foster interdisciplinary collaboration between legal professionals, legal project management, best delivery, other business professionals and clients in order to explore new ways of working and create new and innovative products and processes?
With that in mind, we started our journey with Astrid in April 2019, working closely with her through June 2019 and since then further benefitting from and broadening what we have learned and developed together.

3. How we tackled the challenge

a) Kick-off workshop

We met for our first all-day workshop in April 2019. Attendees included best delivery professionals, legal professionals from all practice area groups as well as business

development managers. Following a brief introduction to the legal design thinking method, we agreed on the scope, identified the status quo, where we wanted to go and how legal design could help us get there.

The result of this exercise was as follows:
The right composition of teams and collaboration is and will continue to be the most important component. We realized that we need to become even more agile and flexible and gain more speed in innovation in order to maintain our leading role.

In the course of the workshop, we analyzed the ecosystem in which we operate. The following diagram summarizes the aspects we collectively considered most relevant:

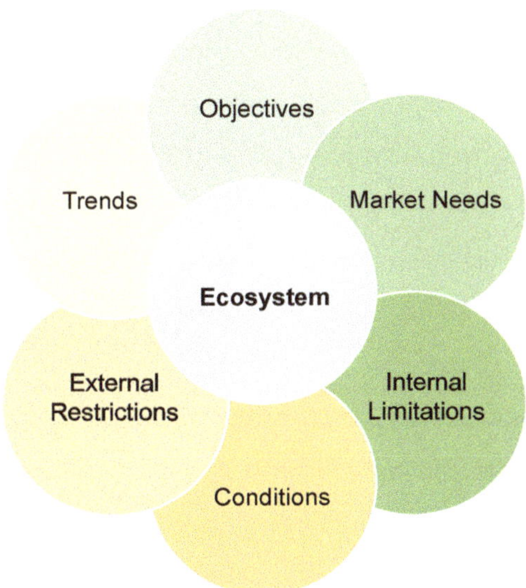

In addition, we undertook a stakeholder analysis to ensure that the Hub's offering is shaped according to the stakeholders' needs.

A brief overview of our stakeholders is below:

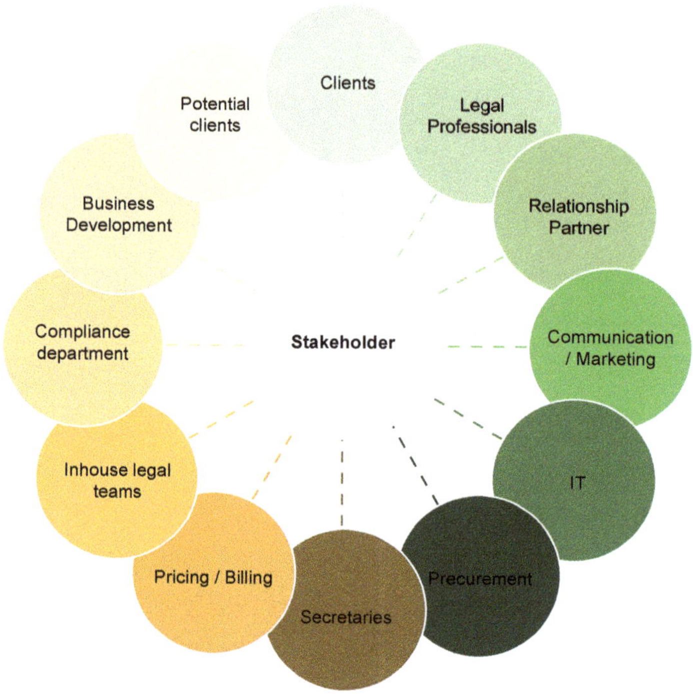

Having determined the ecosystem we were to operate in, as well as the wide range of stakeholders for whose benefit we would be working, we set out to learn about their respective pain points, needs and potential gains. This exercise would in turn enable us to ensure that the services, products and processes we offer would indeed solve our stakeholders' problems and thus increase the acceptance of the Hub and its offerings so that we can drive innovation from within our organization.

Although we thought we had quite a clear idea of what our stakeholders were doing and asking for, we decided to set up interviews with legal and business professionals and by asking the right questions, refine and deepen our understanding with insights into the core of our business. In other words, we wanted to really understand what keeps our stakeholders busy, sleepless at night, what concerns they have and where they see most room for collaboration and innovation so as to better understand their expectations of the Hub.

Having taken this additional step, we knew what we needed to do, how we needed to do it and for whom we were doing it.

b) Stakeholder interviews

We asked for volunteers and selected stakeholders from all our teams – aiming at interviewing legal professionals specialized in different legal areas and a broad range of business professionals from HR, IT, business development and knowledge management functions as well as personal assistants to our legal professionals. In total, we held 45 interviews between April and June 2019 alone and continue to interview in order to gain regular feedback from our stakeholders.

During the initial interview round, we received an overwhelming amount of positive and constructive feedback and a big bag of ideas for innovative projects and future developments. This feedback has been vital to understanding and tailoring how the Hub best creates value for all stakeholders.

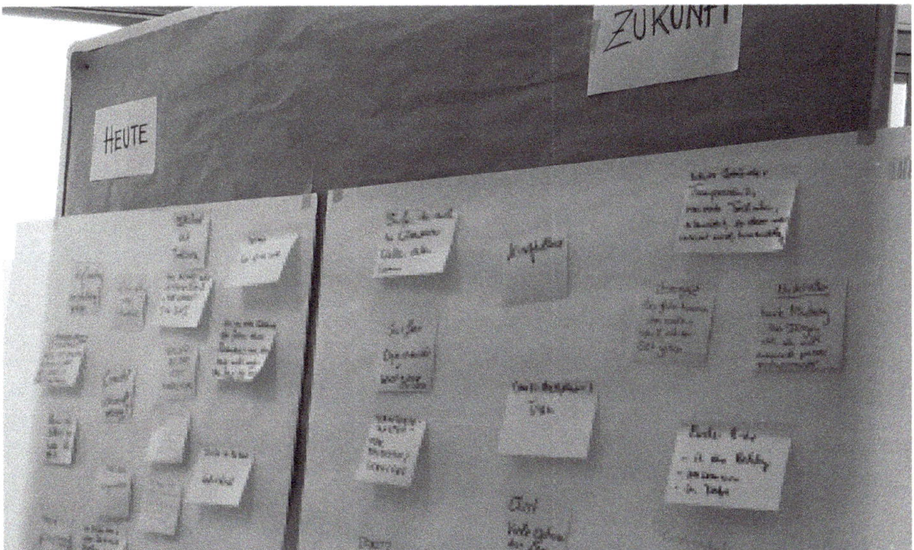

Between gathering feedback and daily business, the team prepared for the physical opening of the Hub space. With colleagues from our offices across Germany as well as from our London hub and other European locations getting together for a big inaugural meet and greet, the Hub officially went into operational mode in mid-May 2019. Dr. Sandra Thiel, Corporate Partner and Head of Innovation of the firm's German operations, commented at the time:

We have created a space for digitalization and innovation right in the middle of one of our offices. This will create a new level of collaboration and creativity to help improve the legal services we offer. We will continue to strive for best delivery and to develop new ideas by bundling our in-house expertise and by working with selected external partners. The integrated Frankfurt Hub is another extension of the Clifford Chance global innovation strategy, which includes further hubs in Europe, Asia-Pacific and the US. The initiative is part of the firm's existing global innovation and best delivery concept which is aimed at developing innovative methods, technologies and ways of thinking for legal service provision.

The opening of the physical space was of course not the end of our Hub going live and gaining momentum. One year on, we continue to refine the tasks and operational mode of the Hub, developing new products and following up on the best ideas collected from our stakeholders' interviews. Some of these ideas have already turned into extensive and productive projects; some are already in the project stage.

c) Analyzing interview feedback

We had scheduled our next legal design workshop for late June 2019. We now analyzed the information collected during the interviews and extrapolated the different pain points. By doing so, we made sure to address the right issues in the Hub's offerings.

We then mapped out a full mandate journey, again discussing pain points, identifying redundancies as an interdisciplinary team bringing together the Hub team with legal professionals from all practice areas and business professionals and external partners. We categorized issues identified in the interviews and developed initial ideas and solutions which were subsequently developed into new processes and products.

As a third part of this second phase, we once again discussed and refined our Hub vision statement following the lead question:

How can we shape the cooperation between legal professionals, business professionals and the Hub team to derive maximum benefit from the Hub for our clients, legal professionals, legal services and products?

We took into account our stakeholders' expectations, such as

- Specific consultation to identify needs and support in transactions
- Short and quick advice to improve daily work
- A place to tackle interdisciplinary pain points
- Sparring partner and idea provider
- Area for brainstorming and developing ideas, regardless of whether technology-driven or not
- Analyze and optimize processes and act as communication and exchange platform
- A forum for questions such as "What influence does technology have on a particular product, task, area?"
- Create awareness/a mindset to welcome change and innovation provided by the Hub increase openness for change management

We then decided on the next steps to ensure we use the input received in the interviews to take the ideas and innovation across the finish line.

4. The result

The result can be broadly divided into three achievements:

a) Hub vision statement: How do we position the Hub within the firm?

Taking inspiration from the input obtained through the interviews as well as from the firm's global innovation and best delivery tagline of "Create. Disrupt. Deliver.",[1] we developed the positioning of the Hub.

Together we...

DEVELOP

...develop innovative, creative solutions and products.

ENABLE

...expand and deepen the knowledge of tools and enable their application.

IMPROVE

...identify inefficiencies and improve existing processes.

In doing so, we continue to expand our leading legal practice.

b) Hub work program: How do we offer our services?

Our thought process and feedback obtained during the legal design thinking process made one thing clear: while it is a prerequisite that all necessary competences are represented in the Hub team and that the team is as diverse as can be, of major importance in making the Hub a success is target-oriented communication to and inclusion of all legal professionals, legal project managers and business professionals, in particular the knowledge management, IT and business development teams.

1 Clifford Chance website: https://www.cliffordchance.com/hubs/innovation-and-best-delivery-hub/innovation-and-best-delivery.html

Starting from a brainstorming idea written down on a Post-it and suggesting "Panem et circenses" as a means to gain additional popularity for our Hub, we came up with a redesigned monthly Hub meeting concept called "TTT," as in Tapas, Tech & Tonic. The concept aims to combine the best of all worlds – intense but open discussion on a given topic, offering a wide range of possible angles and ideas, all set in a relaxed and inspiring atmosphere, including light snacks and drinks, in the Hub.

Other feedback has been picked up, such as the proposal to offer a regular breakfast where news is shared. This turned into a semi-annual practice area-specific breakfast and innovation update. Additionally, we continue to interview through floor-walking (which during the COVID-19 lockdown took place in a virtual format), in particular updating legal professionals on new developments and products, getting them "on board" for specific projects and gathering feedback.

We also increased our collaboration with the business development team to ensure that we are aligned when offering new processes and products, both to our clients and to our legal professionals.

There have been a significant number of individual projects and processes to revise workflows and eliminate redundancies, and we have held workshops with clients on specific projects or digitalization more generally.

One project included a leading global pharmaceutical company asking us to come up with new cooperation models to help it successfully and competitively market substantial portfolios to global clinic operators. The project involved analyzing a broad range of new marketing models on the basis of various country-specific legal requirements. We developed a number of complex models and collated and uploaded the results for each country to our legal tech platform, CC Connect. All involved parties could filter the data by country and conduct feasibility and legal testing on each model. The results were continuously available on an interactive dashboard – reflected in graphics per scenario and automatically updated. This allowed the client and the Clifford Chance teams to analyze the pros and cons of each model in real time, thereby accelerating the progress of the project.

c) Ideas for the future: Innovation projects and quick wins

Another valuable result was the collection of a large number of creative ideas that we retrieved from the interview sessions for projects aiming at new offerings or improvements of existing services.

Among those, a significant number of quick wins and ideas have already been implemented, such as automation of certain templates for which we had not seen the business case before, the creation of a fine calculator for antitrust infringements, a tool to work on documents simultaneously, etc. More complex projects have been started and are to be launched shortly, such as a further focused M&A process, voice recognition, automatic anonymization/pseudonymization or standard corporate AI-supported due diligence reporting. Additionally, proposals for more comprehensive projects were put to the vote to test their potential success and to prioritize their implementation.

In summary, we noticed a significant increase in interest and requests from clients, legal professionals as well as business professionals, which we believe results from the open and broad discussions and the more visible positioning of innovation and best delivery through the Hub. Also, the fact that our German Hub team and our global legal tech operations continue to grow demonstrates that innovation, legal tech and best delivery are becoming an increasingly vital part of our daily business.

5. Lessons learned

We have learned through the observations of the past months that interdisciplinary cooperation and a diverse skill set are key to asserting ourselves in the current market and exceeding both internal and external expectations for innovation and efficiency.

Regular and open exchange with clients as well as our legal and business professionals is vital for the continued success of the Hub. Running interviews like the ones in our legal design thinking initiative is a perfect start to implementing a culture of welcoming innovation and change. It is necessary to acknowledge that each stakeholder has a different need and must therefore be approached accordingly. Above all, having a great team and being part of a great team is key.

Putting legal design into practice extensively and effectively helped us a lot to develop and implement our concept of innovation and best delivery. Today, the Hub is an integral part of our practice and massively contributes to Clifford Chance's dedicated top-of-market strategy. As our Regional Managing Partner for Germany, Dr. Peter Dieners comments:

Digitalization is changing the rules, for both our clients and ourselves. We don't just want to react to this change – we want to shape it as a leading global legal services firm. Our integrated Innovation Hub for Germany is part of our global network of similar hubs. It will allow everyone in our firm, from any practice area or region, to work together on developing and implementing new ideas.

Dr. Sandra Thiel

Partner and Head of Innovation,
Clifford Chance Germany

Sandra Thiel is a Partner in Clifford Chance's Frankfurt corporate practice since 2000, since 2010 she has headed the firm's Global Hospitality Group.

Working with investors and brands in the hospitality sector, Sandra advises on hotel mergers and acquisitions (M&A) and portfolio transactions, reorganizations, hotel agreements and individual hotel transactions, domestic and cross-border. With a background in corporate and M&A, Sandra has also continued to advise on cross-border and domestic corporate work and M&A transactions.

In 2018, Sandra was appointed Head of Innovation and Legal Tech Germany. In this role, she is responsible for the firm's innovation and business change strategy in Germany, which is part of the overall Clifford Chance initiatives. She was fundamental to the foundation of Clifford Chance's Innovation & Best Delivery Hub in the Frankfurt office in 2019. The Innovation & Best Delivery Hub functions as an integrated innovation, digitization and legal tech center applying new ways of thinking, methodologies and technologies to build on and deliver process improvement complementary to the legal advice. As a stand-alone program and by providing a physical space for a permanent core team specialized in legal design thinking, legal project management, legal tech tools, IT, knowledge management and pricing, functions which also form part of Legal Operations, the German Innovation & Best Delivery Hub goes beyond the typical think tank or scrum team, adding value for clients.

Eva Säljemar

Continuous Improvement Project Manager,
Clifford Chance Germany

Eva joined Clifford Chance in 2018 as part of the German Innovation & Best Delivery Team. As a Continuous Improvement Project Manager, Eva improves client and internal customer experiences by streamlining processes and providing advice where efficiency gains can be achieved. For example, she is the main contact to advise on the most suitable best delivery service to use on any particular project, such as using legal project management for complex transactions, collaboration tools or to enhance the due diligence process through the use of adequate legal tech tools. Eva's work is driven and measured by the additional value added to clients beyond and on top of the legal advice.

Eva holds a degree in business administration and is currently pursuing her LL.M. in mergers and acquisitions, which she will complete in 2021. She also holds a Project Management Certificate (Prince 2) and is currently in the process of certifying as a Six Sigma Green Belt. The combination of her business background and her legal knowledge provides her with a profound understanding of the legal business and clients' needs, which is reflected in her work.

Hive Legal: A Case Study of a Purpose-Driven Designer Firm

by

Melissa Lyon,

Associate Principal, Hive Legal

1. Designing a business model

From the very start, design thinking and its required mindsets have played a central role at Hive Legal. Driven by the human-centered purpose of improving the experience for our clients and our team, Hive's founders started with a clean slate. We listened, empathized with, and drew on the past experiences of many users of legal services (clients) and those who deliver those services from traditional legal business models (team). We designed a business model with the attributes needed to achieve that purpose, including a truly flexible workplace, pricing based on value provided rather than time spent, fostering collaboration, agility and creativity, and having the courage to think and act differently.

2. Designing a purpose-driven framework

Designing and building a business model is one thing, providing an approach to identify, design, build and implement ways to improve the experience for users is another. To do this we have developed our own purpose-driven design thinking framework, HiveThink^{P} (the "P" stands for the power of purpose). Because we wanted an approach that truly reflected Hive's culture and purpose, we created our own.

It draws on the essential mindsets required for design thinking, including empathy, collaboration, experimentation and creativity, and provides a framework to:

- identify the purpose and vision for the project;
- use an empathy-based approach to ensure a human centered result;
- assist with building the mindsets needed to sustain change;
- use a multidisciplinary team to ensure the required skills are used for the project;
- design outcomes which will "improve the experience"; and
- ensure that the outcomes can be measured.

It enables our entire team to be involved in designing innovative solutions, overcoming the '"hierarchy-based" mindset that ideas need to come from senior levels or innovation committees. HiveThink^{P} means we start with the problem we are looking to overcome and we focus on the purpose and vision for the project. This assists with overcoming the traditional "silo-based" approach that often exists in traditional law firms, where there is limited collaboration between practice groups, between lawyers and other legal professionals (including technologists, HR, business development and know-how), and between those legal professionals themselves. HiveThink^{P} encourages ideas to come from everywhere and everyone and for everyone to take part in designing the outcome.

By establishing the purpose and the vision of each project, we are able to build in the necessary processes to gather the data (both quantitative and qualitative) we need to measure success and the value of the project supply.

We continue to iterate the framework and how we use it. Based on feedback, we found that while some people like a "brainstorming environment," others would prefer to have more time by themselves to formulate their ideas. So we iterated the HiveThink^{P} process and developed a chatbot (Bee Purposeful), which we built on the Josef chatbot platform. Bee provides the opportunity for people embarking on a design project to gather their thoughts on what they see as the problems they are trying to solve, the purpose, values and vision for the project, and what types of skills are needed. It provides the initial basic platform to "think."

3. How we use HiveThink^{P}

All of our team understands the framework, and we regularly use it to develop and implement ways to help us at Hive and to assist our clients.

User-centered service offerings – HiveGC+

Shortly after Hive was founded in 2014, we recognized that many of our clients required a solution for legal resourcing and assistance that reflects the varying nature of their business needs.

To understand their business-as-usual (BAU) corporate and commercial needs, we asked our clients what they found helpful or unhelpful, what they valued and what they didn't value.

They told us they valued:

- continuity of service
- cost certainty, including fixed prices
- access to a diversity of skills
- commerciality
- access to senior people
- flexibility
- innovative solutions
- resourcing for overflow

Based on what our clients told us and what we had experienced and observed in the past, we designed our HiveGC+ offering to provide:

- a central contact point with servicing from a team of legal professionals, from paralegals to principals at a fixed cost;
- a team committed to getting to know and understand their business at no additional cost;
- the ability to flex the team to their needs in terms of availability, size and skill set;
- access to creative thinking about ways to improve processes and operations;
- resourcing support with a choice for virtual, on the ground (or a mix); and
- regular check-in points so they can try out different arrangements as their needs change.

We continue to iterate the offering and now include working with clients using HiveThink[P] to design process improvements for them, including better contract approval processes. We also use a matter management platform, Xakia, to support the service and provide data to assist the iteration process.

Human-centered process design for a digital health provider

We worked with HotDoc, a digital health provider, to evaluate their privacy policies and processes in order to determine whether they were doing everything they could to provide a human-centered approach to privacy compliance that is transparent, patient-friendly and easy to understand.

Similar to Hive's purpose of "improving the experience for its clients and its team," HotDoc's stated purpose is "enabling the best possible patient experience and improving health outcomes for every patient."

We also share the ultimate goal of avoiding unnecessary legal jargon and creating legal documents (including privacy policies) that are clear, straightforward and transparent for end users.

We considered HotDoc's key internal and external stakeholders and focused on what matters to them from a privacy perspective. We then worked through how HotDoc collects, uses and handles data. Once we had a deeper understanding of this, we were able to look at HotDoc's approach to privacy compliance in a more holistic way.

HotDoc engaged us to work onsite so that we could really understand the products and services it provides and the way that its business operates.
This deeper insight helped us to ensure that privacy considerations and implications were really being worked through proactively across many stages of product development, implementation and operations.

HotDoc valued having a privacy specialist onsite and actively invested in making sure privacy considerations were on track, as this provided a unique opportunity to engage in a really practical privacy compliance review. As a result, HotDoc made a number of changes to the way they handle privacy, including revised privacy policies and terms of service that are more accessible and clearer. This includes adding callout sections in the Terms of Use that make it simple for clinics and patients to understand what the different sections mean, particularly in relation to the relevant privacy provisions.

We also worked with HotDoc to initiate an educational and awareness strategy through which HotDoc can share its privacy compliance expertise with its customers. This is geared to encourage transparency and collaboration. We created materials that aim to help GPs understand their own privacy compliance obligations and know what they should be doing in terms of obtaining their patients' consent before they share data with service providers such as HotDoc.

Collaborating to design an animated privacy policy

Hive collaborated with August, a design and technology agency, to develop an engaging visual animation, as opposed to a text-based privacy policy. It's an interactive, easy-to-understand legal adventure set at sea, to incentivize people to boldly go where few have gone before... the end of a privacy policy.

The purpose for this project included:

- Improving the experience for August's clients and employees by creating a better way to convey what personal information August may need to collect from them, how it is collected, used, and stored, as well as their rights relating to that information.
- Complying with mandatory legal requirements in relation to the type of information August must include in its privacy policy.
- Improving understanding of this policy for the audience.
- Being bold in creating a legal document that doesn't necessarily follow the conventions of the legal profession.

Throughout the project, we dovetailed both teams' tools and processes to combine legal and technology skills with design thinking to conceptualize and develop a functioning policy. The work incorporates bespoke animation transitions and digital storytelling to better communicate privacy information, while meeting and upholding key regulatory requirements.

By using HiveThink[P] we were able to identify the audiences and their motivations in reading a website privacy policy. These audiences include:

- August's clients, both existing and prospective;
- August's team members, both existing and prospective; and
- other people who may engage with August, including suppliers, contractors, and various other interested parties.

August's digital expertise helped us take the insights we developed through HiveThink[P] and craft a bespoke legal adventure that focused on understanding, ease of use, and different learning styles.

Privacy policies are often too long, too boring, or rely on too much legal jargon to convey their meaning.
The privacy policy caters to different learning styles, different device use, and different levels of comprehension. We also ensured that a "plain text" version of the policy continued to be made available for those who weren't interested in our deep-sea adventure.

The policy was tested on different audience groups throughout design and development, including prospective August employees moving through the hiring process, current August team members and third-party contractors.

Helpful feedback during user testing identified a slight disconnect between the policy words and the custom animations, resulting in speech bubbles being placed next to Fernando, the star character in the adventure, to clearly communicate what is happening on the page and why the reader should spend time in that section of the policy.
August has received regular feedback that the policy is much easier to understand with the visual elements and storytelling approach. It has also become one of the most visited pages on the August website.

The policy was named a finalist in the 2019 inaugural Australian Clear Communication Awards in both the legal and digital categories.

Designing and developing end-to-end internal value pricing

As Hive Legal does not price based on time, we do not use timesheets. We provide our clients with a number of scope and pricing options and agree on a fixed price based on the value we will provide to them. This different way of pricing meant that we had to design an entire internal pricing process that works for us and our clients.

We used our HiveThink[P] framework to design the process. We did this by talking to our clients and team to understand their experiences and what worked and didn't work for them in terms of our pricing approach. We then mapped the pricing journey from the perspective of the client and our team simultaneously. This approach meant that we were able to design a process that worked for both our team and our clients.

The outcomes included:

- establishment of a pricing council to review pricing proposals;
- A standardized process to brief the pricing council via a chatbot, aptly named "Val Ewe," which also enables us to capture valuable data;
- options and scoping templates to provide to clients which clearly articulate the value of the options provided; and
- an education program for the Hive team to ensure an understanding of value pricing principles and practice.

We continue to iterate the process, including developing a chatbot that collects and uses our pricing data and know-how to automate the production of our scoping and pricing options.

Designing future direction

We also use HiveThink[P] to assist clients, other legal and professional firms and committees to identify their purpose, vision and values and to develop human-centered strategic agendas.

This has included assisting a newly formed Consumer Panel of the Legal Services Board + Commissioner of the State of Victoria in Australia, tasked with bringing the consumer voice to the regulation and delivery of legal services, and a newly formed committee of the Law Society of Tasmania, Australia, tasked with identifying strategies to attract and retain early-career lawyers.

Melissa Lyon
Associate Principal,
Hive Legal

Melissa is an innovator committed to helping teams develop purpose-driven, human-centered projects through design thinking. To do this, she draws on many years of experience in legal practice, including as a partner in a law firm. She has also held senior business development roles, including managing BD teams and leading numerous projects and programs at a top-tier legal firm in Australia. Melissa works with Hive Legal, an innovative law firm which disrupted the profession by introducing value pricing, truly flexible work practices and technology-based solutions for its clients. Working in this innovative environment inspired Melissa to develop a very different approach to innovation programs and projects based on a design thinking framework and the power of purpose (HiveThinkP). Melissa is a strong advocate for those with skills other than legal and the vital roles that they play in the legal profession. Her work in this area recently saw her named as the 2020 Innovator of the Year (Individual) at the Australian Law Awards.

Queen Mary University of London Legal Design Program

by

Karen Watton

qLegal Director, Queen Mary University of London

Why do this?

Legal design was introduced to master's law students who had signed up for the qLegal initiative at Queen Mary. qLegal sits within Queen Mary's postgraduate Centre for Commercial Law Studies and is an established student-led law clinic providing free legal advice to start-ups and entrepreneurs. Students develop practical skills and professional mindsets as they work alongside external practitioners to help real clients. More recently, qLegal has expanded its activities to become a broader simulation of an innovative commercial firm. Just as leading law firms are innovating and branching into multi-disciplinary practices offering a range of services, so qLegal is following suit, better preparing law students for life after study and opening their eyes to potential new career paths, including within New Law and lawtech.

Experiential learning programs give context to students' academic studies as they gain a practical understanding of the difference between legal theory and application. Working with practicing lawyers helps develop their networking and communication skills and business etiquette. And the fact that students are delivering services to real clients raises motivation while developing students' commercial awareness.

The impetus to include a legal design program stemmed from qLegal staff members' personal experience of legal practice, legal product development and innovative education techniques. As legal educators, the qLegal team felt they had a responsibility to start laying the groundwork for change, in line with qLegal's mission: to help the next generation of lawyers help the next generation of clients to create value in the world. At the core is an appreciation of the opportunities for new roles and new ways of working within the Fourth Industrial Revolution – in particular, the need for a more emotionally intelligent, collaborative and holistic approach to the application of technical expertise. There is a strongly held belief that legal services can and should be delivered better to benefit everyone, and much of qLegal's focus is on developing students' empathy, self-awareness, adaptability and resilience, in addition to their technical skills.

It was also recognized that giving students a new way of problem-solving, drawing on best practices from other disciplines, would add another string to their bow, giving them a competitive advantage as they start their careers, and opening up the potential for further innovation in the future. There has been criticism that universities

The winning team, "T3AM," getting together to work on their prototype:

L-R: Artemy Ivanyushin, Constanca Cruz Ferreira Nunes, Niki Agrotou, Tanya Kalyanvala, Wangari Thuo are not doing enough to keep up with current practices in the legal sector, let alone those that may be in place in the next five, ten or twenty years, and Queen Mary's Centre for Commercial Law Studies, including qLegal, is keen to stay at the forefront of legal education and commercial practice.

The setup

The *Design the Law* program covered an academic year, with 20 places available to the LLM students. The successful applicants, from 12 countries, ranged from qualified lawyers to those straight from their undergraduate degrees with little or no work experience. The program is extra-curricular and structured around legal design challenges to build up students' knowledge and experience. Students attended an induction and two introductory workshops on legal design given by the qLegal director, so they had a basic understanding of design thinking.

The first legal design challenge was run in conjunction with F-lex paralegal agency, a lawtech start-up with a longstanding connection to Queen Mary. The challenge was set by F-lex CEO and co-founder Mary Bonsor: to redesign the company's terms and conditions (T&Cs), which are available on its website. Given that law students are primary visitors of the F-lex site as they register for paralegal work, it was an opportunity to have something created *for* users *by* users.

F-lex and qLegal commissioned Meera Klemola to design and deliver the initial two-day educational workshop. Students were taken step-by-step through the stages of design thinking, and Meera drew on her experience to share practical examples of legal design, bringing the concepts to life. At each stage, the students were set exercises to apply the learning to their practical challenge of redesigning the T&Cs.

The students had been spilt into four teams; they were competing to have the winning team's prototype design adopted by F-lex. In most cases, students did not know each other, so they had to learn how to negotiate a way of working effectively with

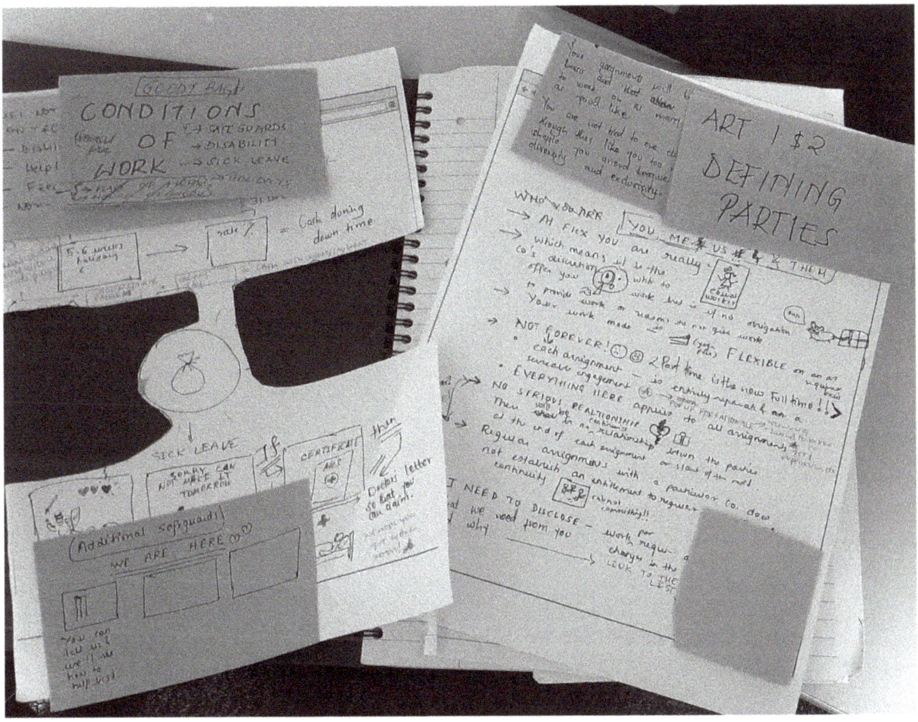

strangers using a methodology that challenged their ideas of being a lawyer, within a competitive framework and with a very tight deadline.

The first day of the workshop outlined the end-to-end process and saw the teams making their first forays into conducting user research interviews – including on each other – creating personas and roughing out tentative prototypes. Day 2 enabled them to carry out further research, ideation, prototyping and user testing, underlining the strong message that legal design is an iterative process. Meera was on hand throughout, answering questions, giving guidance and providing initial feedback. The students also valued being able to gain clarity on the scope of the brief and test ideas with Mary, and gained further insights into the process and feedback on their methodology from Steven Chambers, the UX designer for F-lex.

The workshop was intensive. The students gained enough knowledge in two days to enable them to develop their work over the following two weeks before pitching their prototypes to F-lex's panel of judges.

Observing the students

At first it was a challenge for some students to move away from ingrained ideas on how to think like a lawyer. They had to embrace ambiguity, "silly" ideas, and not aiming for a perfect solution straight away – instead taking time to fully interrogate the problem, empathize with *all* stakeholders, and appreciate that there were many possible answers. Some found it hard to move away from the printout of the T&Cs and

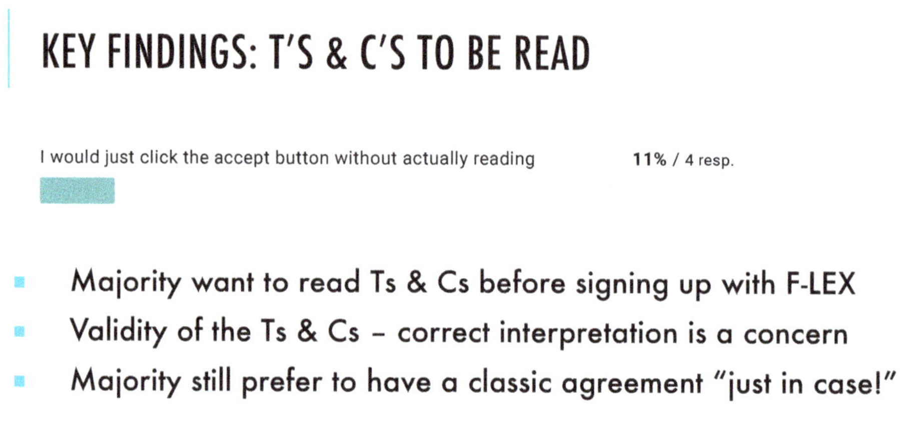

***T3AM* survey findings**

the temptation to make this just another legal redrafting exercise. They were comfortable with the familiar, and it felt risky to open up to a more creative approach.

There was also initial reluctance to share ideas across the whole group, and in particular, to let other teams see first prototypes and give constructive feedback. Mindful that this was a competition, students were concerned that others would steal their ideas, so the suggestion that wider collaboration would raise everyone's game went against their instincts.

What was immediately clear was the high level of engagement shown by all the students. qLegal is used to running interactive practical sessions, but this was exceptional in that the team had to ask the students to leave at the end of each (9 am – 5pm) day despite the students having worked flat out, including in scheduled breaks. It highlighted the difference between extrinsic and intrinsic motivation. There was no grade attached to this, but the students were highly motivated to produce a tangible, real-life outcome for their client and were genuinely curious about what the design thinking process might uncover.

Students' reflections

This was a pilot program for qLegal, and many of the students later admitted they weren't wholly sure what they had signed up for. The program's name – *Design the Law* – and the phrase "legal design" were interpreted by some as relating to policy drafting. Notwithstanding this, all but one of the students stayed the course for the F-lex challenge.

Many students commented in the workshop that it did not feel like work. Students enjoyed problem-solving and giving and receiving feedback in a constructive way as they built on each other's ideas. Meera's "round robin" exercise to facilitate this process was particularly popular, and students who are already qualified lawyers said they would incorporate this technique into their practice.

The most common theme from the students was how their eyes had been opened to the benefits of open collaboration and group working. They remarked that too often in professional practice and in legal studies, they were used to individual output and a competitive mindset as the default. Working so closely with others from different cultures and backgrounds was a breakthrough, as was realizing that collaboration among competitors can achieve better results.

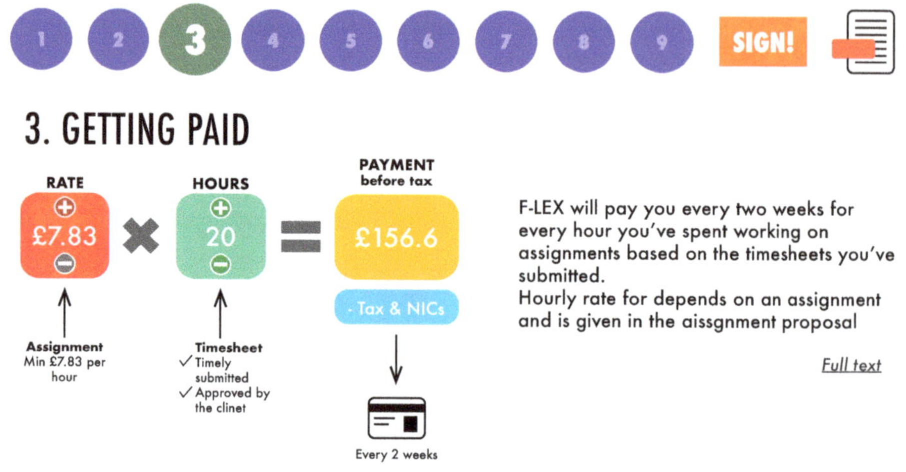

A page of T3AM's prototype

The client's view

Even before the final pitch, Mary received immediate insights and feedback on the look and feel of the F-lex website. In particular, students flagged that the site did not convey the company's warm and human approach, which the students had sensed from engaging with Mary. Students also questioned aspects of the user journey. Some information that was considered important to all users was only accessible once prospective paralegals had been taken on by F-lex – and what happened to the data of those who were not accepted?

The F-lex judges reported being "blown away" by the amount of work the students had put in to deliver their prototypes for the final pitch. This was especially impressive as the students had exams during the project. The teams had all come up with original ideas that improved the existing design, and between them had conducted interviews with more than 250 end users in developing and testing their ideas, enabling them to give a clear rationale for the decisions they had made.

The teams had taken different approaches to the redesign, playing to individual members' strengths without jeopardizing the overall coherence of the product or end-user needs. Prototypes included the use of a journey metaphor with travel-related graphics so that users could easily navigate the site; prioritizing images over text and organizing and layering information, giving users choice on how much they accessed; using humor and an interactive quiz to make sure users understood the T&Cs; and including practical tools such as a salary calculator based on user feedback that salary and type of work were areas where users found existing clauses ambiguous.

There was also variation in pitching styles: low-fi paper versions of wireframes proved to be effective at conveying the redesign, although one student had capitalized on their tech skills to create a prototype website for their team.

There could be only one winner, and the team with the handy calculator took the top spot.

The takeaway

The qLegal team delighted in seeing the students realize they were capable of more than they thought possible. Their confidence grew as they took on tasks that were new and sometimes uncomfortable, and there was an evident shift towards a growth mindset and away from the binary "success or failure" approach they were accustomed to and that can be the block to true innovation. Many expressed surprise at their own creativity: they had previously shied away from defining themselves as creative because they "are lawyers and can't draw." They recognize that they have a new set of tools that can be used in legal and business contexts.

Having a real project with real external partners and a tangible goal played a large part in raising the ambitions and performance of the students, while giving the students space to work through problems themselves encouraged a level of maturity and ownership that surprised everyone.

The level of bonding between the students, and their appreciation of that, was notable and a good preparation for a more collaborative approach for the future.

It is hard to see how these outcomes could have been achieved as effectively through other means. As one student said, "[Legal design] is an abstract thing that is difficult to explain without seeing how it works in real time with a real example."

And so...

The second-semester challenge, designed to cement students' knowledge, was somewhat meta: students used design thinking to create a legal design course for next year's cohort.

Several things came out of this pilot legal design program:

- The students became fans of legal design and practical challenges. They are keen to "hand over" to next year's students.
- Some students have applied for legal innovation and product development roles.
- They have been active in staying in touch with qLegal and with each other.
- qLegal will be incorporating legal design into all its programs, so all students will have access to this additional approach to problem-solving.

Karen Watton
qLegal Director,
Queen Mary University of London

Karen qualified as a barrister and practised law internationally for 15 years, in private practice and in-house. Recognising that the legal profession had scope to improve, she developed an interest in the Future of Work and the Future of Law through senior roles in Careers Consultancy and within the legal tech and publishing group, LexisNexis.

Karen is now the Director of qLegal, the award-winning pro bono commercial law clinic supporting start-ups and entrepreneurs, within the Centre for Commercial Law Studies at Queen Mary University of London. qLegal's mission is to help the next generation of lawyers help the next generation of clients, with a focus on developing postgraduate law students' skills for innovative legal practice and making the experience of law better for everyone. It is the students who, having received extensive training, deliver the free services to qLegal's clients under the supervision of volunteer lawyers from leading City firms.

While studying for her degree in Fine Art Karen started combining law and creative practice, interested to see what was possible when thought processes and outputs from these differing disciplines met. She continues to explore the possibilities through the work of qLegal students on Legal Design-led projects for clients.

AIRBUS – How to Create a User-Friendly Non-Disclosure Agreement (NDA) for Start-Up Companies

by

Astrid Kohlmeier

A special field of applying the legal design method for innovation can be found in the area of contract design. Contract design in general includes the redesign and/or improvement of an already existing contract or the drafting of a new contract.

Such a project can have a much deeper impact than initially expected. The reason for this is that not only the content of a contract itself is being changed, but it is also made more accessible and formulated in a more understandable way. A contract redesign project can also massively push legal organizations, such as law firms or legal departments of companies, towards an innovative mindset. This can lead to a fundamental change in behavior, restructuring workflows and ways of approaching legal problems in general. The phenomenon of real change caused by a redesign contract project happened at AIRBUS Defence and Space GmbH (in the following: AIRBUS) as follows:

The Challenge

AIRBUS has for some time been pursuing the goal of optimizing internal contract processes. One major reason for this goal is, as in many companies, the challenges and new opportunities of digitalization.

According to a 2015 study by World Commerce and Contracting, a loss of 9.2% of revenue in most of the companies[1] was caused by insufficiently optimized contract management. AIRBUS therefore installed a so-called "contract innovators team" with the aim of improving the contract system by using analogue and digital possibilities more efficiently. In many parts of the legal and contract area, solutions for this are being developed in order to gradually improve.

User-centric NDAs for start-ups

The contract innovator team initiated a special project in 2019 with start-up companies as business partners. Fresh ideas from these partners are very interesting for AIRBUS. Very often, start-ups lack proper legal organization or experience in dealing with legal issues in general, especially if a legal department is not yet established. Nevertheless, the first contact with AIRBUS usually includes the signing of an NDA, and for this, a considerable amount of time is needed to complete it on both sides. This is especially true in the case of start-ups, which frequently have no experience with legal issues, and often they have to buy in external legal advice.

In order to find innovative solutions for this problem, AIRBUS's project manager, Ines Curtius, initiated a legal design project, inviting external project leads Lieke Beelen (from the Netherlands) and myself.

1 "Ten Pitfalls to Avoid in Contracting," World Commerce & Contracting, https://www.worldcc.com/Resources/Content-Hub/View/ArticleID/3972

Step 1: Kick-off workshop, stakeholder analysis and deep user research

First, the legal designers introduced the method to the team, and the team conducted an analysis of all the stakeholders in the process of concluding an "NDA for startup companies."

This first step is necessary in every design project in order to determine which internal and external parties involved in a task must be taken into account. The circle of stakeholders is always very broad, and this project began internally with the legal department, individual employees of the contracts department, IT managers, sales managers plus other employees – and of course also extended to the potential business partners (start-ups). After the team mapped out all the stakeholders, comprehensive research of the respective needs in the NDA context followed with one-on-one telephone and live interviews with representatives of all stakeholder groups.

The meaning of "research" in legal design projects

In general, research is one of the most important parts of every (legal) design project. Only structured and analytical research enables the evaluation of relevant insights. These insights are crucial for finding the real, sometimes underlying problem that actually needs to be solved. In most cases, the original, assumed problem does not match with the findings about user needs that intensive user research uncovers.

This was exactly the case in the NDA project: while the contract innovator team in the initial workshop assumed that start-ups would not want to go to the trouble of dealing with legal matters such as NDAs at all, our research revealed a completely different picture. In the interviews, start-ups expressed their fears about their own intellectual property (IP) being transferred to a global organization like AIRBUS and said that the IP would not be sufficiently protected. They expressed their desire for a clear and understandable NDA that shows respect to smaller companies and wished for trustful communication on an equal footing.

At the same time, they complained about many aspects of commonly-used NDAs:

- Too much legalese
- Too much protection of the environment of established companies compared to their own
- Too many complicated, sometimes unfair regulations
- The need to seek external legal advice in order to understand the content of an NDA (especially if an in-house legal department does not exist yet)

Insights:

The research uncovered some major insights about what start-ups really need:

- They want maximum protection for their ideas.
- They have little confidence in the proper handling of confidential information.
- They wish to continue to have control over their IP and ideas.
- They want to know exactly where their confidential information is going when dealing with a big organization.
- Most NDAs do not cover their major concerns.

Interim conclusion:

An intensive examination of users' real needs prevents an organization from solving the wrong problem! If the contract innovators at AIRBUS had followed their first impulse, for example – not to conclude any NDA in the future at all with potential business partners from the start-up scene – they would have completely missed the real needs of the company owners.

Step 2: Design vision, ideas, prototype, test and iteration

The evaluation of the findings led to an intense discussion about the desired design vision, which was to include and align all of the corporation's existing guidelines (e.g., brand guidelines, regulations in contracting, IT guidelines, etc.).

Defining a design vision is always recommended, and this should be used as a basis in subsequent brainstorming sessions. New ideas for solutions have to be embedded into the overall context of the respective company and must not deviate from it completely.

With the aligned design vision, and based on the insights, the main focus was to develop ideas about what kind of NDA would be best the first time AIRBUS came into contact with business partners. It was important to take into consideration what start-ups really want: to build trust, protect confidential information on both sides and be transparent with everything connected to it.

Prototypes

Based on these principles, first prototypes were co-created by analyzing usual and existing NDAs. The whole structure and wording were examined in detail and reworked. Specifically, the prototypes included:

- Simpler language.
- Shorter sentences.
- A question and answer model.
- A simple-to-access structure.
- Visual elements to supplement complicated passages in the text.

Another prototype was developed to turn the NDA journey into an interactive, digital experience, with the help of an intuitive, easy-to-use application that covers the entire NDA process. The app should be ready to use in the first conversation and make it possible to close the contract live and in real time.

Test and iteration

The prototype design was followed by a user test with the previously defined relevant start-ups. The testing of the various prototypes delivered essential findings – for example, which passages were easily understandable and which were not, what effect the agreement had on the users and what emotions the process evoked in them. Based on the test results, the prototypes were improved again several times before arriving at a final version. You can see the final version of the Word-based document on the next page.

Results and effects of a legal design project on the organization

Besides the improvements and the confidence-building aspect of concluding the new NDA, the project described above also led to remarkable changes within the internal organization. Not only is AIRBUS now redesigning other contracts step by step based on the legal design approach, but the contract innovators have also gained more and more visibility within the global company. Participants in the first design project reflected on the lessons learned as follows:

Interdisciplinary cooperation and change on the project

Through the integration of all stakeholders in the process, the team naturally took a multidisciplinary approach to the project. What in other contexts often runs rather cumbersomely worked without hurdles here, because each of the parties involved felt that their interests were represented. Concerned parties became participants – a goal that is a central topic in every change management project.

In addition, the NDA project achieved great recognition within the company and also gained high visibility outside (e.g., through the use of social media). It also contributed to the company-wide goal of being an innovation driver in the market.

It is remarkable that the innovation project did not come – as usual – from the product department, but rather from the area of legal and contracts, a circumstance which in itself is already very unusual. For this project, the contract innovators director, Ines Curtius, received the 2019 World Commerce & Contracting Innovation & Excellence Award in the category of Strategic Achievement.[2]

2 World Commerce & Contracting website, https://www.worldcc.com/

Advantages of simplified and user-friendly contracts in general

Legal design projects have a relevant impact and deliver payoffs on important key performance indicators (KPIs):

1. Reduction of the processing time

Simple-to-understand and accessible contracts lead to a reduction in processing time for all parties. There are fewer approvals and questions on the part of both contracting parties. The time required for the initiation of business – e.g., in the area of sales as well as on the side of potential business partners – is less, which leads to a fast exchange of information, but also to measurable cost savings. Innovation in the

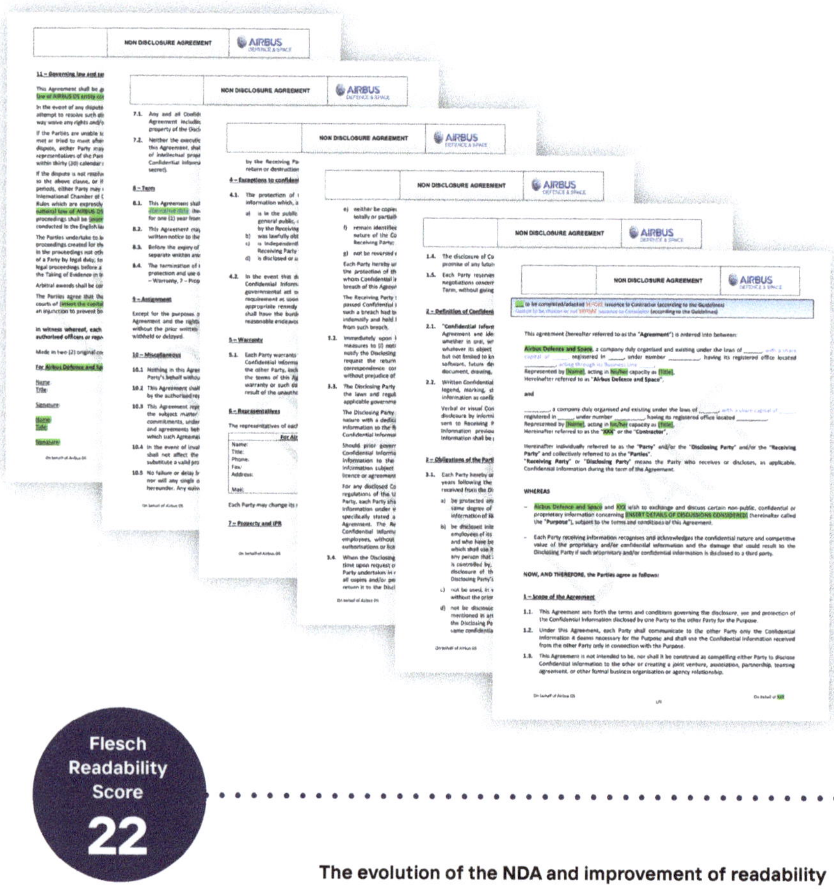

The evolution of the NDA and improvement of readability measured with the Flesch Readability Score.

form of contract design remains an unusual signal to customers, business partners and employees, but it can also make a measurable contribution to the transformation of traditional legal entities into cost-oriented business units.

2. Machine readability even of AI-based tools.

In the age of AI-based contract analysis tools, one may ask whether a simple and visualized contract leads to restrictions. But you can rest assured: even with the addition of visual content, SEAL software was able to successfully analyze the described NDA on the first try without any specialized training.

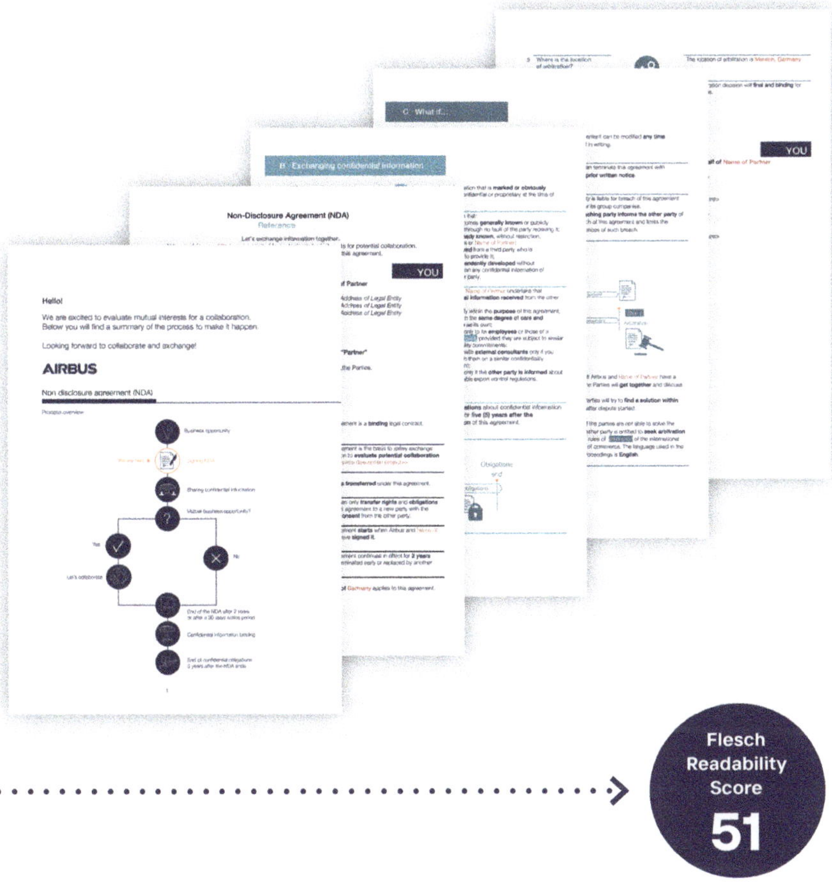

Flesch Readability Score
51

Conclusion

A contract design project leads to contracts that are more accessible, intuitive, transparent and efficient. In addition, it contributes to internal change towards innovation and a generally more innovative mindset. An interesting observation: the parties involved did not experience such a change project as a burden. The feedback from the project participants made clear that they not only gained new skills and knowledge through the new method, but also had a lot of fun during the joint workshops and project. A contract design project leads to a better understanding of the real needs of other stakeholders and supports a consistent, positive team spirit. Besides, after participating in such a project, working in a multidisciplinary team is no longer a foreign concept, but a real experienced advantage that will also be useful for future challenges.

Legal Design for an International Bank - Beyond Redesigning Contracts

by
Angélica Flechas,
CEO, Háptica
Andrés Polanía,
Account Leader, Háptica
Jorge García,
Legal Leader, Háptica

1. Challenge that the project aims to resolve: legal design project

Every single day, people access services to perform different kinds of tasks and achieve certain goals, whether it be buying a house, asking for financial advice or even getting a loan. Taking this into account, we could say that it is impossible to find an aspect of life that is not affected by a service. At Háptica, the first 100% Colombian service design consultant agency, we have spent the last six years designing services of every kind. Over the years, we have found that even though a brief at the beginning may not have directly included legal design, during the development of the project we found legal design opportunities in many scenarios. Much like in the case of services, it is impossible to find an aspect of life that is not affected by a legal touchpoint that could be redesigned to better suit users' needs.

During this project we engaged with the bank's legal area; they were looking for a company who could help them with the redesign of contracts to make them easier for their clients to understand. The legal department was very concerned about the legal effects of modifying the documents – a situation which has traditionally led to lawyers becoming reactive thinkers to mitigate any possible risk. However, in many cases this perspective does not allow us to think about the user experience across the different existing legal touchpoints.

The project took place at Bancolombia, the largest bank in Colombia, with over 11 million clients. The corporation has a special interest in client experiences, and their user experience division strongly influences the operation of the whole bank. For this reason, the brief needed to offer solutions that went further than just putting words into clear and understandable language. We needed to connect the user experience of the bank's clients with a business model that could rely on these documents for its success.

The project consisted of redesigning an investment management contract in which a customer could transfer an amount of money (more than USD 2.5M) to the bank to manage their resources. These kinds of financial experiences are part of a service that includes various actors, each with different roles, activities and responsibilities. The delicate and fragile relationship between these actors must be built on trust rather than fear or mistrust. It is also important to point out that the problem to be resolved was not only about legal documents, it was also about the user's tasks, goals and above all, the story of the user. Taking all these aspects into account, it was clear that the solution had to come from the field of legal design.

The method applied was:

A. Research

B. Analysis

C. Co-creation

D. Prototype

E. Mentoring

F. Evaluation

2. How did we tackle the challenge?

A. Research

When talking about design thinking, the most important part of the methodology is truly understanding the needs of the end user in order to create a final solution that fulfils those needs. When talking about service design, this approach requires recognition of the user experience as a complete system in order to identify innovation opportunities in the design of the touchpoints that make them come to life.

However, when talking about legal service design, not only do we need to understand the user needs and the complete experience, but we also need to make the legal structure that coexists in the story fit with the complete context of the situation and ensure that the final result is legally applicable.

The first phase of the methodology applied on this project was Research; this phase required an understanding of the complete context of the experience that we wanted to improve. To facilitate the process, we created a pyramid (figure 1) to visualize the different levels of the explorations along with a toolkit of different research instruments to cover all its levels of complexity.

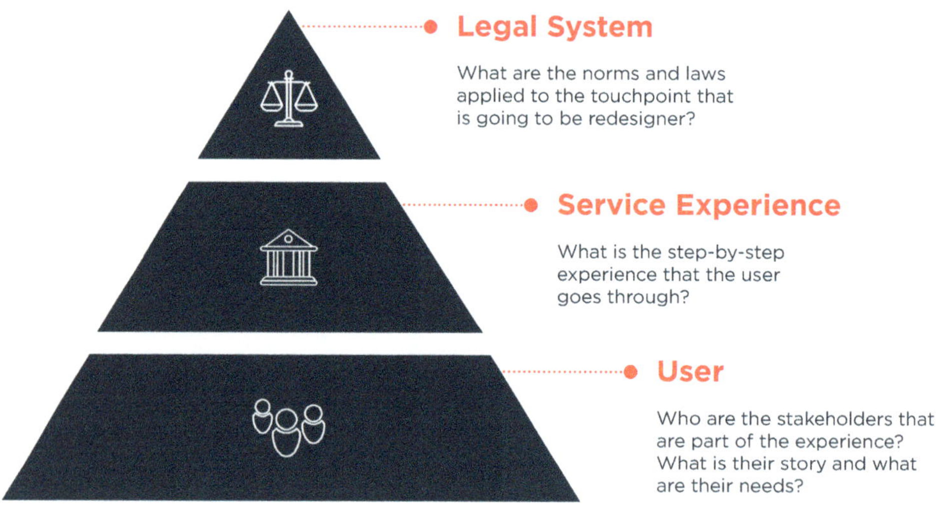

Figure 1. **Pyramid of research**

In this particular project, for the legal system level of the pyramid, we gathered all the regulatory information related to the contract with our legal mapping tool. In this workshop, all the lawyers involved put together a list of the laws that must be taken into consideration. Both public laws and regulatory information from the bank were gathered. This input was crucial to redesign the experience at the end of the project.

During this phase, we also checked the document itself using our *Heat Reader Tool*. This tool applies basic computational linguistic principles in order to achieve an analysis of the grammatical characteristics and vocabulary. The process identifies the density and complexity of each of the clauses that make up the legal document to then define the rhythm of the document. This is a key concept to analyze the user experience with the legal content: by counting the number of paragraphs, counting the words per sentence, and identifying their syntax, it is possible to generate an index (Figure 2) for each clause and thus be able to map the structural form of the entire document.

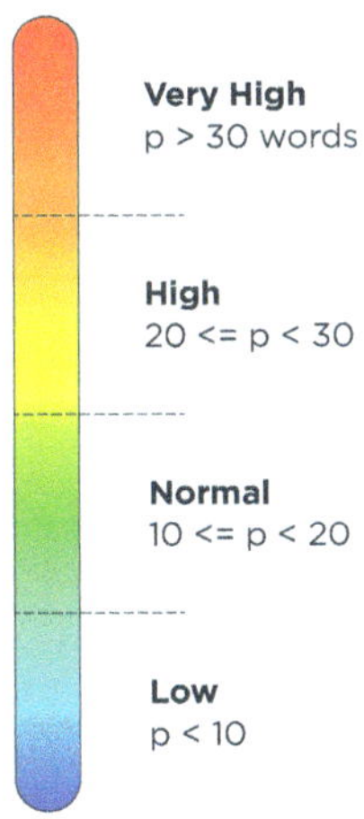

Figure 2. **Index of complexity**

After exploring the legal system, we moved on to the next level of the pyramid: service experience. To understand this component, we met with key stakeholders from the bank to discuss the complete journey of the product and the main points of the story. We interviewed clients, sales team members and legal leaders of the bank with the aim of mapping all the touchpoints: channels, people, spaces, processes and objects that were relevant to the experience. One of the legal touchpoints was the investment management contract, so the results generated by the Heat Reader Tool were taken into consideration, and only the most complex components were used; the complete document is too long to expose to the user.

The last level of the pyramid is the users. It was important to really get to know the clients, the sales team members and the legal leaders of the bank related to this product, because redesigning the contract affects the experience of presenting, negotiating and closing the deals associated with the stock commission contract. We acted as observers during the commercial process and then discussed the experience with the commercial stakeholder to explore any doubts and variations in the process.

B. Analysis

Although we have been implementing design thinking and service design for six years, this project was different. This project had a clear legal component, and we had to ensure that the topic was covered in our analysis. During this process, our goal was to organize information and cross-reference content to identify insights, although the main challenge was finding the legal implications.

Certain tools were crucial in facilitating the process. The first main tool was creating a customer journey map with legal insights. This provided the structure to organize the findings regarding the complete experience and the role of the contract in each moment according to a customer journey timeline.

C. Co-creation

This step of the methodology was essential to establish two key elements in the project process that generate the construction path of the legal document design. The first element is the beginning of the creative process for building the documents and finding innovative elements for the context, and the second but equally important element is how we use the input from the users to understand what they need and expect.

To accomplish the first objective of this step, we needed to explore cutting-edge solutions and new ideas applied in other areas to see which could be applied to this project. To achieve this, we gathered all the information that had been collected and analyzed in the previous steps of the methodology related to the needs and applications of the document. This meant selecting insights that impacted directly on the narrative, order and/or intention of the document (concepts mentioned before). A great way of doing this was compiling the insights and connecting their opportunities with legal design patterns and real context solutions. By doing this, we could observe design elements or solutions that had previously resolved similar issues.

To accomplish the second objective, we prepared a workshop intended to give users – and a strategic group of stakeholders who were invited to the session – a set of tools chosen to trigger divergent thinking and invite them to explore a new concept of use for the document and the intention that it presents. The tools and steps for this crucial workshop were selected from the Háptica resources, in which we have constructed and adapted a variety of legal design thinking activities/tools to help people co-create new ideas and possible solutions for legal contexts (figure 3).

Figure 3. **Workshop co-create**

This workshop allows us to accompany users and stakeholders while they bring to life a new concept of use for the document and determine the intended interaction between users and the document. The result is a totally new meaning for the document, much more than just a legally binding agreement.

D. Prototype

During this phase of the methodology, various legal prototypes were constructed to define design determinants and goals for the project. Prototyping sessions were held to evaluate the form and content of the document; lawyers, commercial stakeholders, users related to the business, and non-legal users were all invited to participate. In one session, the group of lawyers quickly recognized the advantages of the new document. On the other hand, the initial reaction from the commercial non-legal user group was negative because they thought that the new document was not a legal document. We realized it was necessary to update their understanding of contracts; the group needed to understand that contracts aren't just black and white Word files with a 9-pt font size, but also an instrument of negotiation.

E. Mentoring

After building the document prototypes, we entered the Mentoring phase, in which we worked with people who have contact with the document. An essential requirement for the project was the design of an "operable document" for relevant actors who will modify or manage the document. These actors are mostly lawyers who do not have training in design and who usually only use basic word processors. This was a great challenge for our project designers, because they do not usually design processes with the aim of the final result being managed in basic word processing programs.

Evaluating projects born from an innovation perspective can be very difficult, because the effect can impact multiple dimensions of the service. For this reason, we defined the key performance indicators (KPIs) to be used to measure the impact of the new contract. We proposed three levels of measurement indicators to understand the impact of implementing this human-centered methodology. The first level of indicators focuses on measuring the legal touchpoint of the contract itself. The second level covers measurement indicators specifically related to the legal process. The third level measures users' complete and holistic experience (commercial and legal) when interacting with the service and its legal and non-legal touchpoints.

F. Evaluate

The final result was a document built natively in Microsoft Word and the definition of a legal design system inspired by the current design system of the bank. This bank is the first to have exclusively created a system composed of assets for the construction of legal documents: a set of reusable components that align under a series of guidelines and that can be grouped in different ways to devise any legal document. The bank is currently processing the validation of this system.

3. Images – Results

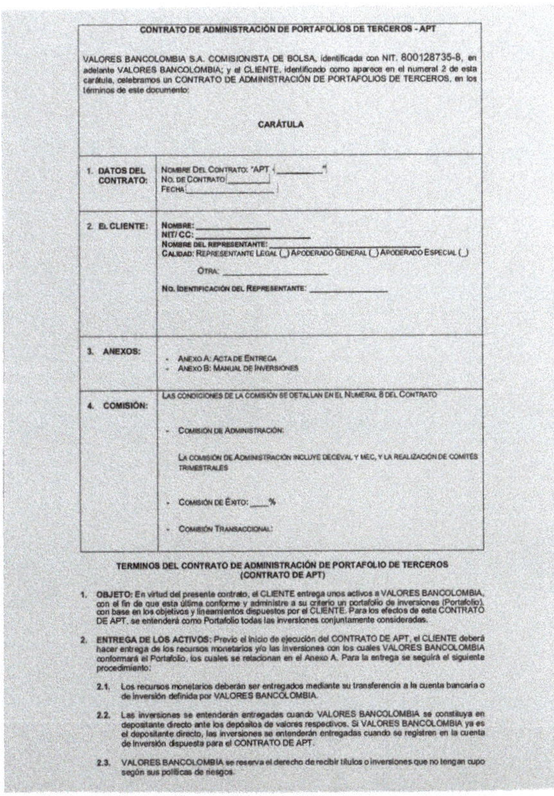

CONTRATO DE ADMINISTRACIÓN DE PORTAFOLIOS DE TERCEROS - APT

VALORES BANCOLOMBIA S.A. COMISIONISTA DE BOLSA, identificada con NIT. 800128735-8, en adelante VALORES BANCOLOMBIA; y el CLIENTE, identificado como aparece en el numeral 2 de esta carátula, celebramos un CONTRATO DE ADMINISTRACIÓN DE PORTAFOLIOS DE TERCEROS, en los términos de este documento:

CARÁTULA

1. DATOS DEL CONTRATO:	NOMBRE DEL CONTRATO: "APT - ____" NO. DE CONTRATO ____ FECHA ____
2. EL CLIENTE:	NOMBRE: ____ NIT/CC: ____ NOMBRE DEL REPRESENTANTE: ____ CALIDAD: REPRESENTANTE LEGAL (_) APODERADO GENERAL (_) APODERADO ESPECIAL (_) OTRA: ____ NO. IDENTIFICACIÓN DEL REPRESENTANTE: ____
3. ANEXOS:	- ANEXO A: ACTA DE ENTREGA - ANEXO B: MANUAL DE INVERSIONES
4. COMISIÓN:	LAS CONDICIONES DE LA COMISIÓN SE DETALLAN EN EL NUMERAL 8 DEL CONTRATO - COMISIÓN DE ADMINISTRACIÓN: LA COMISIÓN DE ADMINISTRACIÓN INCLUYE DECEVAL Y MEC, Y LA REALIZACIÓN DE COMITÉS TRIMESTRALES - COMISIÓN DE ÉXITO: ____% - COMISIÓN TRANSACCIONAL:

TERMINOS DEL CONTRATO DE ADMINISTRACIÓN DE PORTAFOLIO DE TERCEROS (CONTRATO DE APT)

1. **OBJETO:** En virtud del presente contrato, el CLIENTE entrega unos activos a VALORES BANCOLOMBIA, con el fin de que esta última conforme y administre a su criterio un portafolio de inversiones (Portafolio), con base en los objetivos y lineamientos dispuestos por el CLIENTE. Para los efectos de este CONTRATO DE APT, se entenderá como Portafolio todas las inversiones conjuntamente consideradas.

2. **ENTREGA DE LOS ACTIVOS:** Previo el inicio de ejecución del CONTRATO DE APT, el CLIENTE deberá hacer entrega de los recursos monetarios y/o las inversiones con los cuales VALORES BANCOLOMBIA conformará el Portafolio, los cuales se relacionan en el Anexo A. Para la entrega se seguirá el siguiente procedimiento:

   2.1. Los recursos monetarios deberán ser entregados mediante su transferencia a la cuenta bancaria o de inversión definida por VALORES BANCOLOMBIA.

   2.2. Las inversiones se entenderán entregadas cuando VALORES BANCOLOMBIA se constituya en depositante directo ante los depósitos de valores respectivos. Si VALORES BANCOLOMBIA ya es el depositante directo, las inversiones se entenderán entregadas cuando se registren en la cuenta de inversión dispuesta para el CONTRATO DE APT.

   2.3. VALORES BANCOLOMBIA se reserva el derecho de recibir títulos o inversiones que no tengan cupo según sus políticas de riesgos.

Figure 4. **Before the redesign of the investment management contract**

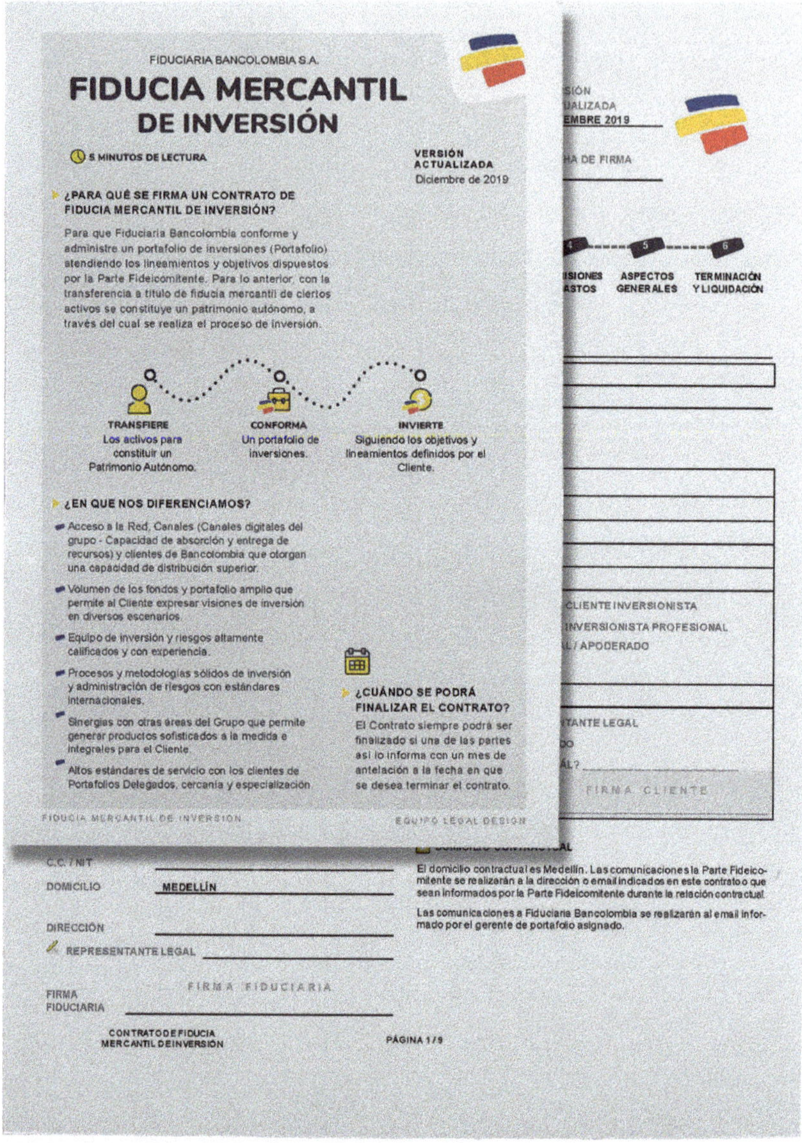

Figure 5. **After the redesign of the investment management contract**

4. Reflection

What worked?

The successful development of this project was made possible by a variety of elements, but the most important element was the client's philosophy. This bank is known for being the most innovative bank in Colombia; they had already established a culture of innovation that created new systems and challenged older systems in the bank, but they hadn't previously applied it to legal aspects. In this case, the legal department themselves initiated the project, so we didn't need to convince them to change their processes or legal touchpoints because they already knew it was necessary.

Nevertheless, we needed to include the product owners because the documents and process that were going to be redesigned belonged to product areas that weren't already aware of the project. We made sure the product owners were present from the beginning of the project in the discovery phase until the prototype stage.

What didn't work?

One of the most important and difficult components of a legal design project is the impact and how that impact can be measured. In this case, our direct contact for the project was the legal team, but one of the tools that we wanted to use to understand the impact of the project was surveys with the bank's end clients. However, the commercial department, to whom the clients belong, didn't want to involve their customers in our research in the final step of the project for one of the documents that we had designed because of the profiles of those specific clients.

What is the most important thing we learned?

Even though the name "legal design" seems to indicate that this method only applies to the legal aspects of a company, our approach is more holistic. Through this experience we realized that legal service design covers legal components that are touchpoints in a broader user experience. This means that the changes affect not only the legal part of the organization but many other departments, too, and so data collection should be a priority for all the areas involved.

What is the current impact for the bank?

We worked so closely with the client in the legal area during the development of the consultancy that now they call themselves legal designers. Since the completion of the project, the legal team of the bank has redesigned 25 other documents with the support of legal innovation leaders who emerged during this process. Some of those initiatives have required approval from Colombia's Superintendencia Financiera, the regulator in the financial field, and the new legal touchpoints have been approved without hesitation.

Furthermore, we are facilitating an academic program for 20 lawyers from the bank in order to show them how legal service design goes beyond documents and how it can also improve processes, experiences, products, systems and mindsets.

This method has broken boundaries, and now that we have finished our first project there, we are eagerly awaiting the next challenge.

Angélica Flechas
CEO,
Háptica

She is a Lawyer and Designer from the Universidad de los Andes and is currently studying an Executive MBA at Hult Business School. She is also the founder and general manager of Háptica, the first consulting firm in Colombia dedicated to designing services and implementing Legal Service Design methodologies. Thanks to her double profile, she has been able to develop initiatives with law firms and legal departments of Banks and Insurance Companies, being one of the pioneers in this field in Latin America.

Andrés Polanía
Account Leader,
Háptica

Computer and Systems Engineer and strategic Designer, with experience in Service Design consulting, social context mapping and software development applied to real problems for people.
His specialty is the facilitation of conversations through methodologies for the development of projects with a focus on the legal user experience, technology and its interfaces.
His main interest is the study of the intersection of the humanities with new technologies that promote legal innovation processes, inclusion services and more humane.

Jorge García
Legal Leader,
Háptica

Lawyer and legal design passionate, has worked in Law Firms, Legal Departments and Public Organizations, while adopting innovation mindsets and methodologies to the legal practice and its teams. Currently, he has been working at Háptica as Legal Leader, supporting the Legal Service Design projects of the organization with his legal expertise and giving them insight in the methodology.

Engaging Non Profit Organizations in the Financial Action Task Force Debate

by

Lieke Beelen,

CEO, Founder, Visual Contracts

Andrea Montella Lavin,

Legal UX Designer, Visual Contracts

1. Challenge

The Financial Action Task Force (FATF) is an organization in charge of creating and implementing policies to combat threats to the international financial system, such as money laundering or terrorism financing. Among the stakeholders involved in these regulations we can find Non Profit Organisations (NPOs), which are susceptible to suffering from these types of threats and which, as a consequence, have strong regulations that block their daily operations.

One of the resulting challenges from the policies implemented by the FATF is that NPO's cannot easily open a bank account or that essential international transactions made by an NPO are blocked. The transaction may be a valid transaction in order for the NPO to do their good work. For example, a task of an NPO might be that they provide blankets in emergency situations which are dependent on payments for logistics to transfer the blankets to the right location. Delays in financial transactions might delay the delivery of the blankets in time for the winter season, missing the purpose of the NPO's mission to help people in need.

This happens because of the preventative approach that the FATF regulations take, in which NPOs have less capacity to adapt to FATF regulations (mainly due to resources) compared to the ability of other entities such as banks, governments, the FATF Coalition and the UN. A solution would be to distribute the risks and efforts to prevent money laundering and terrorism financing from happening among all the parties in a more balanced way and in proportion with their capacity. Nevertheless, in practice NPOs are currently carrying the costs of these highly regulated policies.

As a result of this issue, the Global NPO Coalition platform was created in order to support NPOs in coping with the FATF regulations. Additionally, they also intend to involve NPOs in a more proactive way in the creation of the regulations and recommendations by the FATF. Human Security Collective (HSC) was the organization responsible for the redesign of the Global NPO Coalition's website. We as Visual Contracts collaborated with HSC and a development agency (Hamaka) on the website redesign project.

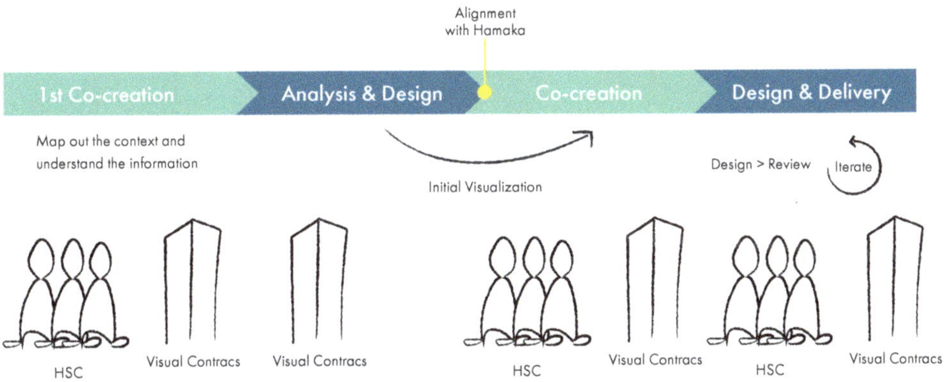

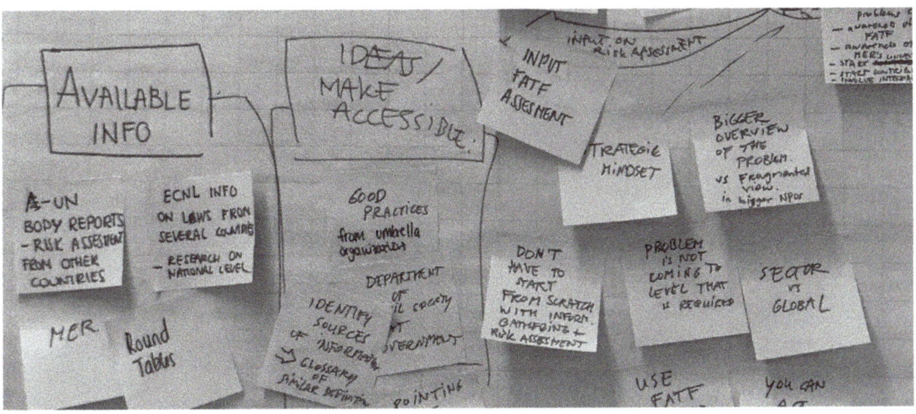

The purpose of this project was to help stakeholders – but specifically NPOs – understand the FATF regulations and to help them engage in the debate on counterterrorism financing (CFT). Our mission was to help HSC synthesize, structure and visualize the information, and also to find the right media (visualizations, interactions, animations, etc.) to communicate this information on the website.

2. Approach

First we conducted a co-creation session to map out the context and to also to get a better understanding of the information. This session was divided into two parts. The first part was with HSC, wherean overview of the context, the stakeholders' roles and their relationships was established. In the second part, in which there was representation from several stakeholders, the focus was on mapping out the journey that NPOs go through,to highlight the main pain points they must overcome and to identify possible solutions to these issues. Finally, we defined a design vision about what we wanted to achieve with this project.

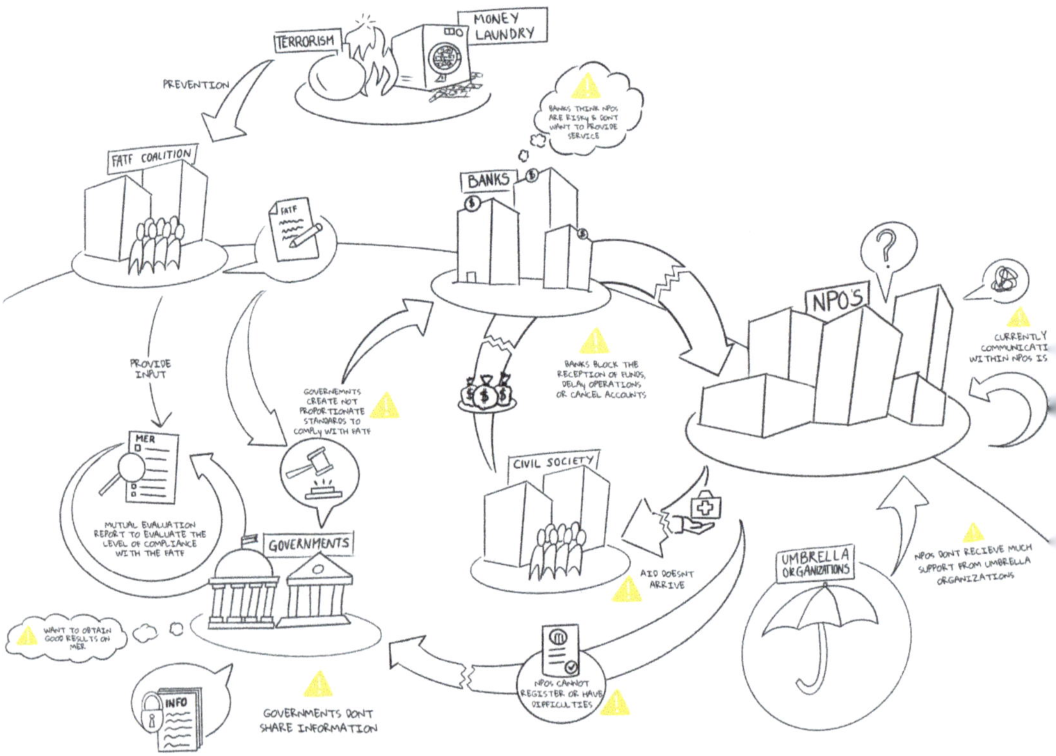

Afterwards, we analyzed and clustered the information to find the main topics among all the information that needed to be communicated. Using these clusters, we started the visualization process, beginning by mapping out the context. Mapping the context helped us to draw all the relationships between the stakeholders involved. After creating some initial sketches that showed the context, the issues and solutions to these issues, we began the second co-creation session.

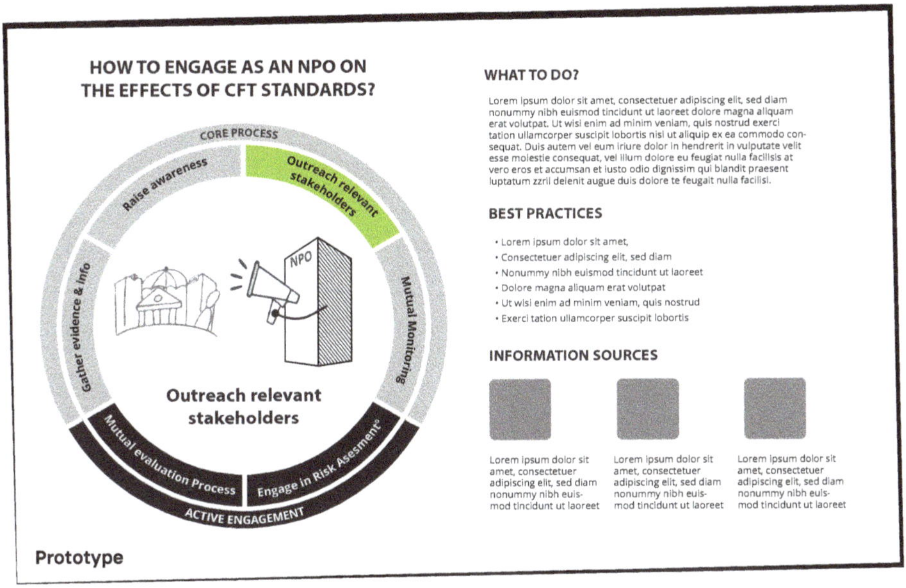

Prototype

The goal of the second session was to make sure that the information in the sketches was correct and fill in any possible gaps of missing information. Using the sketches as the base, we created new visualizations in collaboration with the client and defined any additional visualizations that were necessary.Finally, we defined the style of the visualizations and the type of interactions that would be created, always advising the client and looking at usability.

The next step was to create the first interactive prototypes, first as wireframes. We introduced the changes and then went through several iterations with reviews from our client to create all of the specific content.

Finally, when all the content was ready, we styled it according to our previous discussion and in line with the designs provided by the development agency. After a couple of iterations to find the right way to represent the stakeholders and draw the relationships, we delivered the interactive prototype.

3. Outcome

The outcome was a series of different visualizations that focus on the journey of NPOs. We decided that the best way to explain the whole story was to explain the context, the main issues NPOs encounter and possible remedies that would help to alleviate these pain points. Set up like slides, these visualizations use the context as the reference and show the interactions and roles of all the stakeholders, making it easy for the user to follow the story.

Another important part was the engagement of the NPOs in the dialogue relating to the CFT. The goal was to provide clear steps and resources for the NPOs to be more engaged with the CFT. This visual is interactive, and it is possible to click through the different phases, making the information for the NPOs clear and quickly accessible.

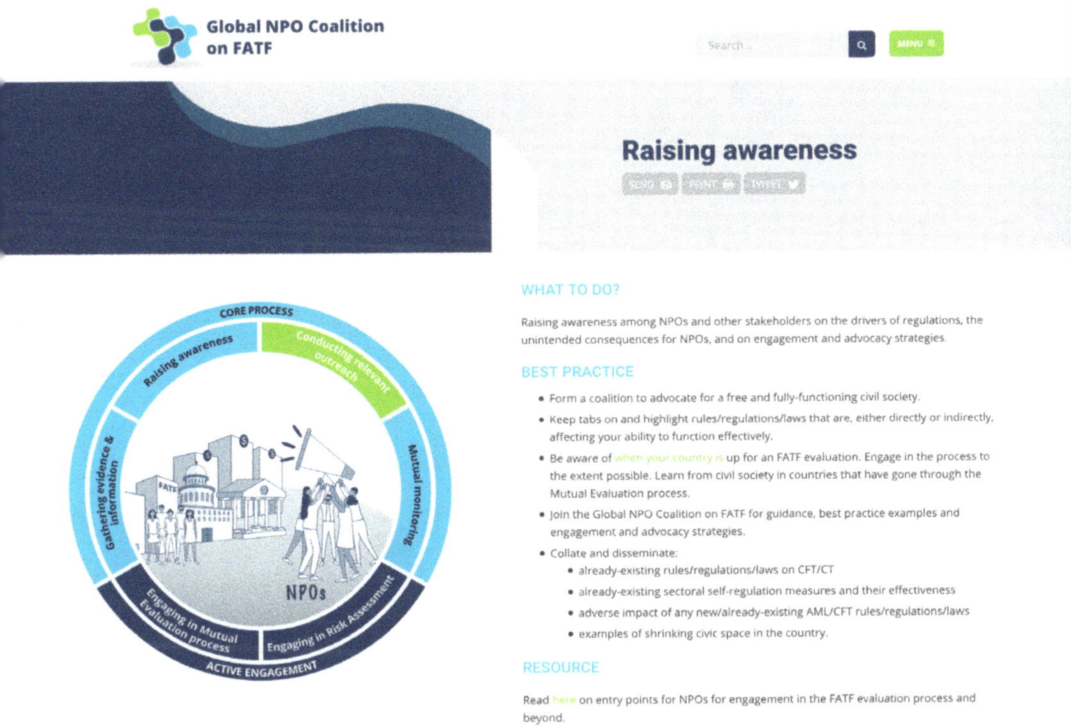

Personal reflection by contributors

It is important to be involved in the design from an early stage. We were a bit limited when choosing the medium for the design, since the responsibility for the development of the website was with an external agency. Our involvement came a bit late to the project, when all of the designs were ready, and we had to adapt our legal information design to the pre-existing visuals. Additionally, due to budget limitations we could not design a completely interactive prototype, and instead we had to limit ourselves to images and very small interactions.

Nonetheless, the client was very positive about the results. The redesign of the website including our visuals was also received positively by their visitors. This was also evidenced by the increase in newsletter sign-ups after the new website launch.

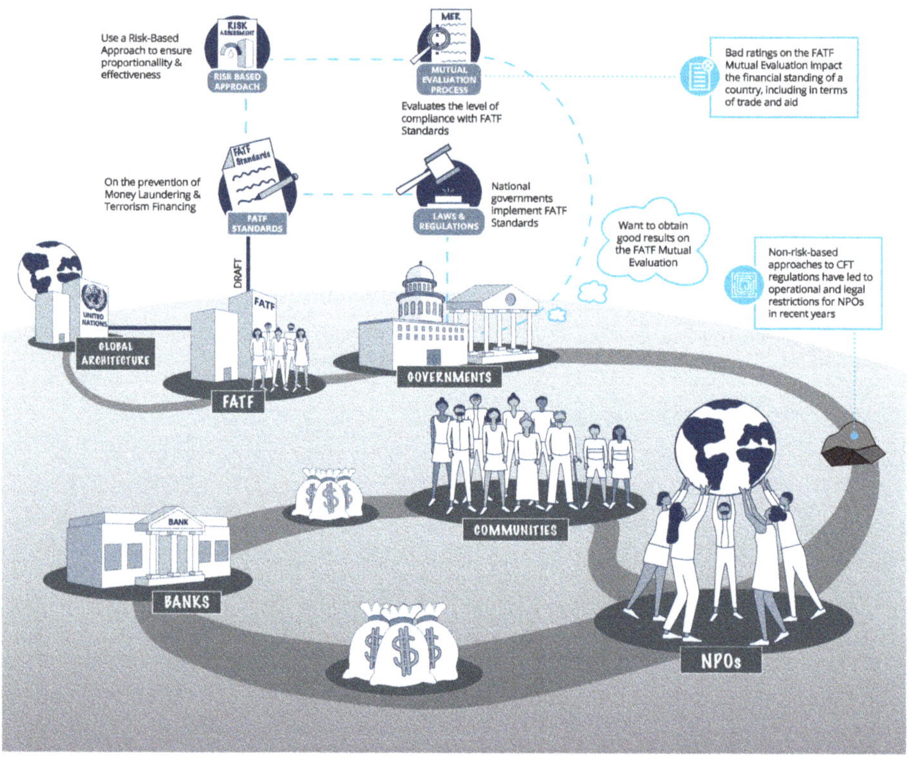

From our own perspective, we saw that the client was involved in the process and was impressed about what we could do with visualization to make complex matters easier to understand using just simple sketches and the co-creation approach. They had worked with consultants and students before to tackle the complexity of the topic, but didn't have similar results. We ourselves also got to learn more about the Financial Action Task Force and the situation regarding the way these regulations can actually block good intentions on the part of NPOs. Here you see how overregulating – for an understandable goal – can also harm good initiatives and place the responsibility for these international challenges onto smaller organizations. There is still an opportunity to apply more legal design in the collaboration between different, bigger bodies in order to solve the shared responsibilities regarding international risks and threats.

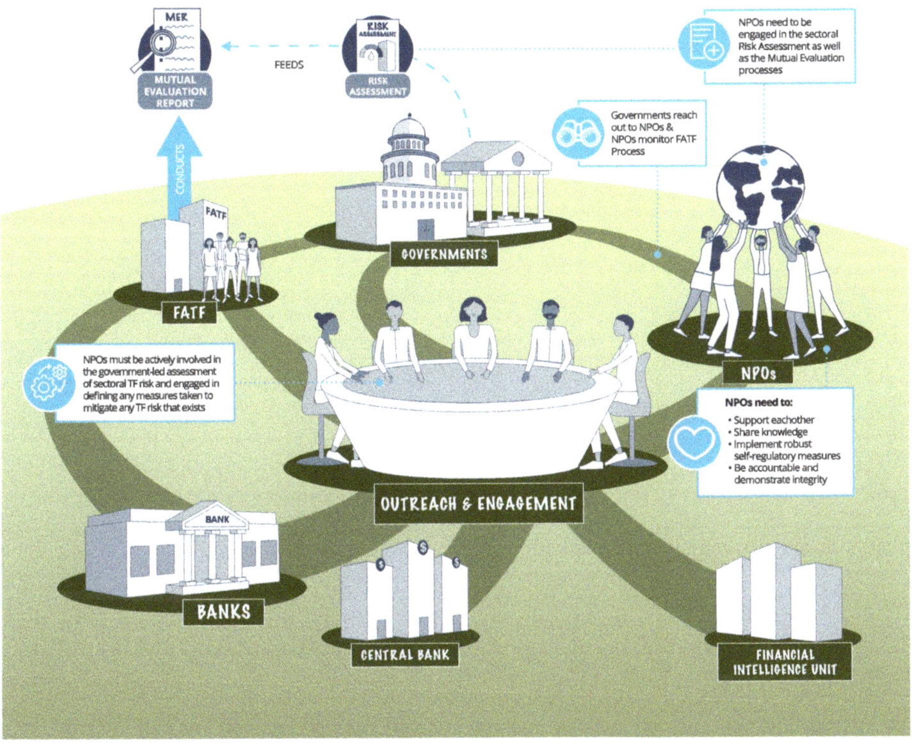

Lieke Beelen
CEO,
Visual Contracts

With a background in industrial design engineering (MSc. in design for interaction at Delft University of Technology) Lieke has worked as a service/UX designer and researcher in many different contexts. Since 2015, she has focused on the legal sector, to create access to law and access to justice by facilitating lawyers and designers to work together from a legal design thinking perspective. In June 2017, she launched the platform Visual Contracts, which offers all the tools and materials needed to learn how to create visual contracts. With her team, she is now developing a visual contract builder that makes visual contracts more accessible to a broader range of people.

Andrea Montella Lavin
Legal UX Designer,
Visual Contracts

Andrea is a Spanish-Italian industrial designer, specialized in UX and interaction design. Since 2017, she has lived in the Netherlands, where she works as a legal UX designer for visual contracts. She has a passion for design and a natural curiosity for human behavior and complex societal problems. For this reason, Andrea's mission as a designer is focused on creating meaningful solutions that generate social impact using experience design. Andrea came across legal design while working on her MSc thesis at TU Delft, when she was looking for a way to pursue my passion for social design. Andrea immediately started working with Visual Contracts, focusing on the topic of fairness in employment contracts. From that moment on, Andrea became engaged with the legal field, which is often both challenging and rewarding for a designer. During this time Andrea came to realize that design, when combined with other disciplines like legal, becomes a catalyst for change that can create positive impact and help to change society.

www.legaldesign-book.com/links

Want more homework?

There are many more great examples of Legal Desgin out there in the wild. It would be impossible to keep this up to date here, so kindly visit the above website for a list of links to some of our other all-time favorites.

See you there!

Chapter 5
Field Work

Chapter 6

The Role of Legal Designers

6

The Role of Legal Designers

Chapter 6
The Role of Legal Designers

We have described why legal design plays a major role in the context of the current transformation in law and how the method can be implemented in practice. We already know that innovation and design require a certain mindset and strategic foundation so that they can be systematically adopted in legal organizations.

But we also want to focus on those who are in charge of innovation and possess the empowering tools for conducting legal design projects. This chapter is therefore about the people who lead innovation projects and in particular, about the role of legal designers now and in the future.

Legal design is in itself a new and evolving profession, so we need to look at what skills a person needs to have in order to fill that role properly.

We want to approach this new professional role in two ways:

→ From a skill set and professional model point of view.

→ From an organizational point of view.

Which professional profiles currently exist in the legal industry?

Let's take a look at established professional profile models and find out if and where legal designers, with their unique set of capabilities, might fit in.

I-shaped personalities

The so-called I-shaped expert is characterized by the fact that they are particularly well versed in one field, but less or not at all in other fields.

Peter Connor describes the I-shaped lawyer as someone with profound traditional skills and legal knowledge and a smaller portion of business knowledge and soft skills.[45]

In addition to this model, there is the generalist, who is not a specialist in any subject, but who instead has broad knowledge of several subjects. This profile does not represent a true specialization, but generalists can often point out, evaluate and benefit from good cross-connections between different subject areas.

X-shaped personalities

The X-shaped professional is characterized by the fact that working in a multidisciplinary environment is particularly easy for them. The X-shaped professional is also a master of collaboration. These X-shaped professionals are necessary in the field of design thinking and are becoming increasingly important in general. This is due to the overwhelming and widespread recognition that multidisciplinary working skills are what will be required in the future workplace – ultimately leading to better solutions.

T-shaped professionals

We also find so-called T-shaped professional profiles, which were strongly propagated by IDEO founder Tim Brown. He describes T-shaped professionals in the field of design in the following way:

> *The vertical stroke of the "T" is a depth of skill that allows them (T-Shaped professionals) to contribute to the creative process. That can be from any number of different fields: an industrial designer, an architect, a social scientist, a business specialist or a mechanical engineer.*
> *The horizontal stroke of the "T" is the disposition for collaboration across disciplines. It is composed of two things. First, empathy. It's important because it allows people to imagine the problem from another*

45 Connor, "The T-Shaped Lawyer"

perspective – to stand in somebody else's shoes. Second, they tend to get very enthusiastic about other people's disciplines, to the point that they may actually start to practice them. T-shaped people have both depth and breadth in their skills.[46]

The T-shaped professional is a profile that has been referred to for some time in the legal sector, as a way to illustrate the future skillsets for a lawyer.

According to Peter Connor, a T-shaped lawyer has multifaceted characteristics that are very well illustrated in the next figure. The figure shows the relationship between traditional legal knowledge and skills that are learned through legal education, and adds many other capabilities a lawyer should have today:[47]

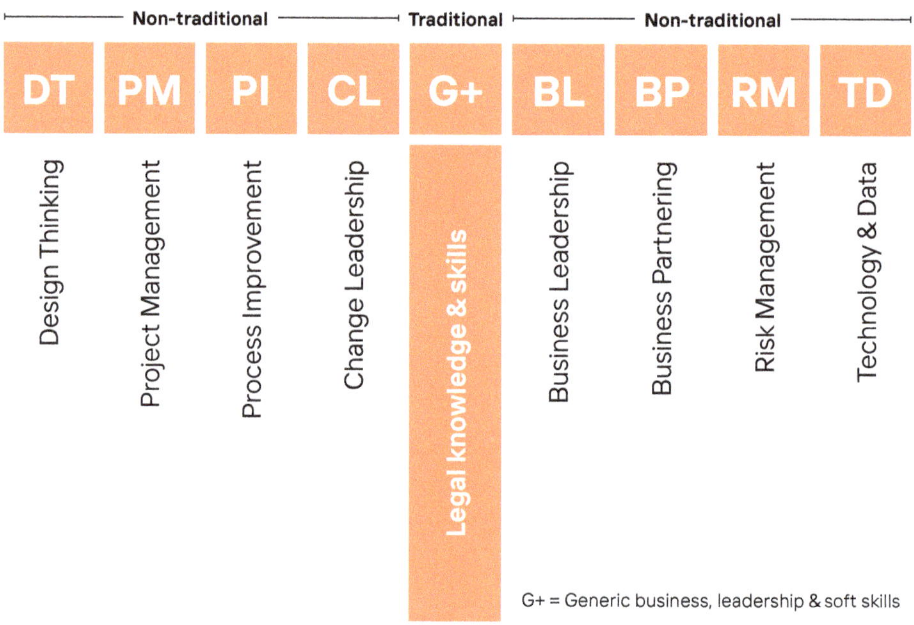

46 Hansen, "IDEO CEO Tim Brown: T-Shaped Stars"

47 Connor, "The T-Shaped Lawyer"

The profile of the T-shaped lawyer illustrates very clearly that traditional legal education alone is no longer sufficient when it comes to performing the role of a lawyer and innovating in the field of law both today and in the future.

Is the T-shaped professional model the right one for legal designers?

What we particularly like about the T-shaped lawyer model is the description stating that lawyers must open themselves up to new skills and fields in order to be able to shape the future of their services and products. One can, of course, wonder which skills are the most important and which ones an already trained lawyer really needs to master. One positive observation is the fact that for the first time, design thinking plays a role in the orchestra of skills that a lawyer should possess. On the other hand, the illustration makes it clear that today's lawyers need to learn several new skills in order to keep up with current developments.

In the context of legal tech, we often hear the question of whether lawyers should learn how to code. There are many people who suggest just that: lawyers *should* be able to code. But be careful! It is not quite as simple as that. If programming is supposed to be the most important skill a lawyer has to learn today, this misses the question of which skills are important for innovation in general. For lawyers who offer many technical solutions, it can be important to be able to do some programming themselves. But look at all the other skills of the T-shaped lawyer model: would it mean that every lawyer who wants to master future challenges should learn several professions in a row? That is probably a difficult and unrealistic requirement to realize.

We want to promote the idea that lawyers today must be able to do one thing above all else: appreciate the added value of genuine interdisciplinary collaboration and actively seek contact with other specialists, professionals and professions. In our opinion, the basis for adopting this new approach is an innovative way of thinking, which enables lawyers to obtain the opinions of other professionals and to broaden their expert horizons by better understanding other experts. A breadth of new knowledge is vital; at the same time, it is essential to recognize the value of working with other experts with deep expertise in fields outside of law – like, for example, coding.

The Delta Model

Let's now take a look at the Delta Model, which was developed by a mixed group of lawyers and academics from different backgrounds. It has now been defined by Alyson Carrel and Caitlin (Cat) Moon,[48] as an agile competency model for the modern legal professional. The Delta Model reflects the holistic and broad variety of skills that are necessary for future lawyers.

The Delta Model follows the principle of simplification, but also takes into account the ongoing changes in the legal ecosystem and emphasizes maintaining its flexibility for the future – that is, the model is in constant evolution. The current state of the model is as follows:

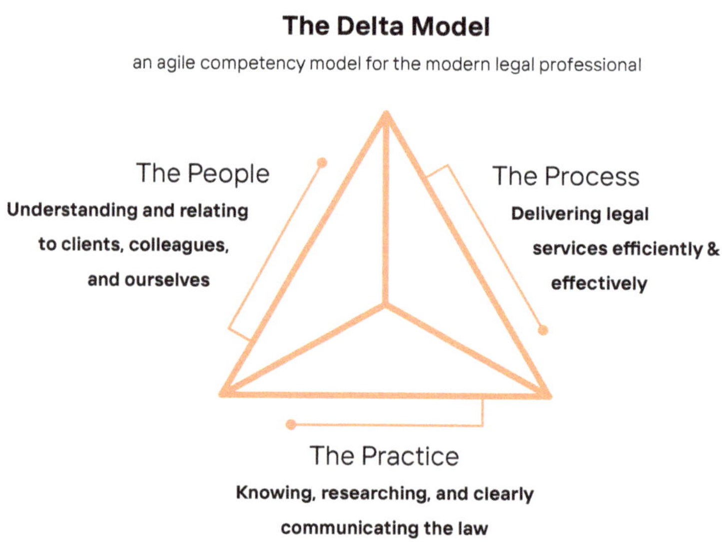

48 Carrel and Moon, "The Delta Model." Alyson Carrel is Clinical Associate Professor of Law and Co-Director, Center on Negotiation and Mediation at the Northwestern Pritzker School of Law. Caitlin Moon is the Director of Innovation Design and Lecturer in Law, Vanderbilt Law School.

What we really like about the Delta Model is the wording and the open formulation that refers to “legal professionals” instead of lawyers only. We especially like the idea that every legal professional should develop an individual set of skills and is not strictly obligated to follow an already fixed model.

Conclusion

Without wanting to evaluate all the different professional models here in detail, there is one conclusion we can draw from the given models for future legal professionals, and that is that there is a strong need to restructure legal education if we are to keep up with the ongoing transformation the world is experiencing. We have to:

→ Overcome the traditional mindset of legal professionals.

→ Offer more diverse training that is focused on more than just material law.

→ Open up to reshaped legal professions.

Now that we have shared some different models of what future professional profiles for lawyers could and should look like, let’s turn to a new profession: the legal designer.

What is the legal designer’s profile?

Let us first start the discussion by exploring what skills a legal designer should have and which qualities are most important in order to make the most effective professional impact.

Second, we want to discuss what value this new type of profession could have for legal organizations and where we could imagine the right position in the different ecosystems.

The skills of a legal designer

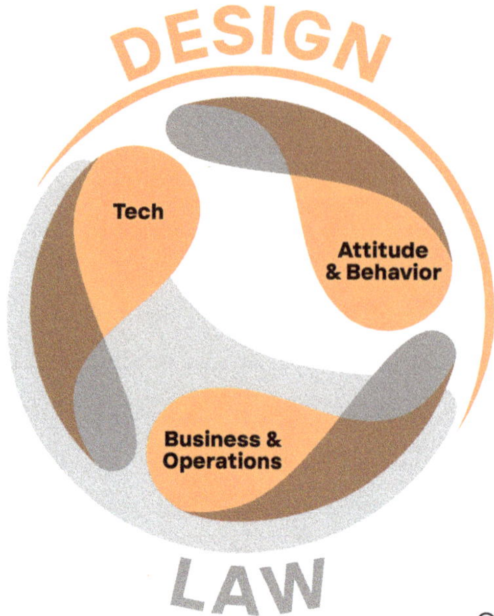

© The Floating Model
by Klemola & Kohlmeier

A legal designer has to bring a variety of skills and education to the table that enable them to perform legal design work. We have created the Floating Model to express the various capabilities that are needed. The capabilities that legal designers require can be grouped into what we call five areas of expertise:

- Law
- Design
- Technology
- Business and operations
- Attitudes and behavior

We discuss each of the five areas of expertise in greater detail below. The idea behind the floating elements is that the depth of professional knowledge and capability under each identified theme can vary, particularly depending on the type of legal design project being done. We should note that the Floating Model, much like the Delta Model, is in a state of flux. This means that the model will evolve over time as the role of the legal designer starts to become more well-defined.

The Floating Model: Five areas of expertise for a legal designer

Law

All legal designers need a profound base of legal knowledge – not only in a theoretical way, but a legal designer should also ideally have practical legal business experience. That said, a legal designer does not need to have a formal law degree, but rather an open attitude to learning and understanding legal specifics; they should bring a deep understanding of legal issues and the perspective of a lawyer.

Without this understanding, it is difficult to appreciate legal challenges, work faster and gain credibility with lawyers. As we stated at the beginning of this book, lawyers have a proven tendency to be highly skeptical. Therefore, an already established background of experience in the law will position legal designers more favorably for collaboration with their lawyer counterparts.

Legal knowledge, practical expertise and (at least) a very deep understanding of law are crucial for every legal designer.

Design

Another must-have skill set for a legal designer is deep knowledge and practical experience in the field of design. As we stated in Chapter 2, design is a broad field consisting of different areas and specializations.

In the context of legal design, we see a particular need for knowledge and experience in the following design disciplines:

- Graphic design
- Service design
- Design thinking
- Product design
- Information design and information architecture
- Communication design
- UX design
- UI design
- IX design

It is almost impossible to have deep expertise in all of those professions, but the magic sauce lies in the combination –– and at least in a very deep understanding of the different areas.

A quick example will help explain why the combination is so important these days: Let's imagine that a legal designer wants to contribute to the innovative development of a legal tech offering. To do so, they must combine several design fields such as graphic design, service design and UX design to deliver a good end product.

As in the professional models we saw above, the key is to make yourself open to deep interdisciplinary collaboration; however, a true legal designer's skill set should include at least ONE design area. Or to put it succinctly: there is no legal design without designers! Way too often we see what happens if designers are NOT added to a project. The outcome is usually only half of the idea that a legal designer could deliver, and it often fails to create a solution around real user needs that is helpful, useful and solves a real problem.

Caution!

Sometimes lawyers tend to easily brand themselves as "legal designers" without taking into account that becoming a designer requires a long-term education, usually in a university setting. A proper design education at university takes almost as long as a legal education. We would therefore like to take the opportunity to kindly warn lawyers to not use the term "designer" too quickly. It may offend "real" designers and undervalue design as a profession as compared to law.

Observations

When starting to build both legal design awareness and legal design capabilities, law firms and legal teams often try to start with their own staff, which is great and understandable. However, since legal design is very new (and currently there are only a few books or educational courses on the topic), what we have witnessed and been told by clients is that initial attempts to build legal design with internal resources alone often fall short. We conclude that this is the result of a lack of materials for people to train in legal design and a lack of a real understanding of what legal design is and how it should be implemented in an organization. Here is a small example of what we mean: if a legal organization wants to re-design a contract, for example, what most commonly occurs is that the task is delegated to an "assistant" who is instructed to "make contracts more colorful." In such cases, the work performed is not legal design, but simply cosmetic touch-ups. Legal design encompasses researching all stakeholder needs, prototyping, testing and getting feedback from real users. So if you are in a legal team seeking to onboard legal design, do consider the value of bringing in an external legal design expert in the first place. This person can train and build legal design competencies among your staff, who will carry out legal design initiatives in the future.

Conclusion

Good legal design requires deep design knowledge and the ability to collaborate with others. These are two of the core capabilities found in every competent legal designer.

Technology

In addition to a legal designer's core skills in law and design, there is also the very important area of tech. We advocate a deeper understanding of technical aspects and propose that practical experience should be taken seriously – at least in an interdisciplinary and collaborative way. For example, we don't see coding as a really necessary skill for legal designers, but a mindset and understanding of the tasks a programmer has to take care of are essential for any legal designer.

If legal designers are not capable of understanding the needs of IT personnel, it might become difficult when it comes to developing ideas with technical components. Especially in an era of legal tech, we see this field as very important. A legal designer should be capable of differentiating between the tasks that are needed in the back end and in the front end – not only from an UI and/or a UX perspective and therefore the designer's field, but also from a technical point of view.

Side note: Embedding law into design and product development

This becomes even more important if we consider how to embed law and legal aspects into the fields of tech and product/service innovations at an early stage. The sooner legal designers are integrated into the pipeline of new developments, the better the outcome will be. Ideally, legal designers should be integrated from the outset or early on. This little example makes the rationale for early involvement by legal designers very tangible: If an automotive company is developing and producing a new car that can drive autonomously, for example, the product development team should consider the potential legal implications of their development right from the start. A real practical example would be to take into account regulations such as GDPR. For instance, a legal designer could easily help to advise product designers on the way a car's dashboard should be designed on both the front and back ends in order to fulfil GDPR regulations. Today connective technology and face recognition are being used in automotive vehicles, and they will be used even more in the future. What if product developers did not take into account that the usage of personal data is part of an individual driver or guest's decision? What if product developers forgot to add a button to the cockpits' interface that says something like "don't use my data in this car"? If there is no button in the design, then it is also likely that no functionality has been foreseen in the back end as to where personal data will be processed and stored. Of course, one could argue that companies would be safe because buyers of such a car usually give consent in the contract at the time of purchase (by the way: these contracts are usually very long and complicated for buyers to understand). But honestly: wouldn't it be better if legal designers could share such important knowledge early on in the product development process?

Conclusion

A deep technical understanding – and in the best case, practical experience and knowledge about the specifics of developing technical solutions – should be part of a legal designer's skill set. The executing of technical aspects itself is not required, but an understanding is essential.

Business operations

It is of utmost importance to be able to place legal design in the context of various operational and business-relevant issues. This can only be done by legal designers who bring business acumen and strategic insight and have dealt with various ecosystems. Legal designers must be able to understand a legal solution's contribution and translate that contribution into how it may affect a company's strategy, bottom line, marketing and image building. They also need to understand how companies operate, what workflows are needed to make them successful, what different mechanisms work together and which challenges companies face. Behind all of this is also the ability to understand complex issues (an asset that lawyers naturally have anyway). But legal designers should not be shy about cooperating with the top management of a company. Understanding project management at management level is essential, because legal design is always about innovation.

We have already learned that innovation requires a strategy that should be embedded in the DNA of a company. Legal designers are people who are not afraid of contact and can permeate complex problems in business.

Attitude and behavior

Legal designers not only need knowledge in different areas; they also need certain outlooks, attitudes and behaviors. The following attitudes and behaviors are important in order to be an effective legal designer:

Collaboration

Legal designers must be able to cooperate with others and have the experience and willingness to share knowledge and learn from others. This is one of the most fundamental requirements: the ability to bring together different stakeholders and people from different professions and both lead and encourage them to work together to develop better outcomes.

Empathy and emotional intelligence

Legal design without empathy and emotional intelligence is impossible. It is crucially important to be able to see, understand and feel different needs and the different emotions certain needs may evoke – and to be able to manage these needs in connection with a legal design task. Putting oneself in the position of others and seeing from others' perspectives is one of the crucial skills that are needed by every legal designer.

Keen communicators

A good legal designer has excellent communication skills. It is very important that legal designers are able to conduct conversations, facilitate dialogue and know how to ask the right questions. Legal designers pair excellent communication skills with the ability to listen both actively and deeply. They then harness their communication skills to convey messages to an audience and build mutual understanding among people.

An innovative mindset

It goes without saying, but it is still worth mentioning that legal designers need an innovative mindset that is open to change! Such a mindset is made up of various components; a nice summary can be found on the Hasso Plattner Institute's website.[49] Accordingly, the main components of an innovative mindset are:

- Think and act in a human-centered way.
- Collaborate in diverse teams.
- Explore the problem space.
- Learn through experimentation.
- Embrace uncertainty.
- Envision a radically new future.

Legal Designers in an Organization

After shining a light on the different skills that are required of a legal designer, we can clearly see that legal designers are a hybrid professional composition. The exciting question now is that of where legal designers are best placed within organizations. Is the legal department the right place, or is legal design a new function in the overall structure of a company?

This question is not easy to answer, and we do not have enough examples at present to show where legal designers have been successfully integrated into companies or law firms. At the moment, the few legal designers that exist worldwide are working either in an academic environment (some of them, like Colette Brunschwig, for example, have been around for decades) or in their own consulting agencies, working as contract visualization experts, or they are still soaking up the information that exists on the subject of legal design.

49 "Design Thinking Mindset for Innovation," Hasso-Plattner-Institut website, https://hpi-academy.de/design-thinking/design-thinking-mindset-for-innovation.html

Let's look at where legal designers could make the best contribution to business success in the legal landscape:

Legal designers in law firms

In traditional law firms that consist of partners, associates, paralegals and assistants, a legal designer probably would not fit in at first glance. But, a legal designer might come into action if a traditional law firm truly wanted to transform its offerings and value proposition. At this stage we would see a legal designer as a long-term external consultant or as an employee who operates at a strategic and senior level.

Traditional settings that want to transform should take this innovation step very seriously, and the sooner a legal designer comes on board, the better. A legal designer will bring a fresh perspective combined with the ability to drive collaboration and support the team with an innovation mindset. A legal designer will also be sure to embed the client viewpoint in each decision.

We know from experience that innovation and change will not happen overnight, so our advice is to let legal designers be true business partners and close consultants or add them to the existing staff on an equal footing with the management or partners.

Innovation is an ongoing and never-finished task and attitude, so if a traditional law firm is willing to change, this should be considered to be the new norm. Change and flexibility in service offerings will accompany successful law firms forever.

Legal designers in leadership positions

Head of client experience

A legal designer in the future could easily hold the position of head of client satisfaction and client experience. They are well positioned to occupy leading roles and open up new functions that collaborate with all the departments – legal operations, legal tech, innovation, marketing and business development. We think the most impact could be made in the function of **head of client experience.** In this role, a legal designer would be the voice of the client, ensuring that every strategy, product or service aligns with the client's needs and demands.

Head of innovation

Another good option for law firms with already established innovation teams is to place a legal designer at the head of such a department. Why? Legal design is all about innovation and combines all the different aspects that are needed to innovate and drive innovation from a strategic and business point of view. Last but not least, it also supports the development of a true, collaborative mindset as the original basis for any innovation and change.

Legal operations manager

With a multidisciplinary outlook combining law, design and business skills such as project management, legal designers are also well suited to legal ops teams.

Facilitators

More and more, clients are seeking to solve legal problems in collaborative ways that use methodologies such as Design Thinking and Agile. Legal designers are skilled facilitators and workshop creators with extensive toolkits in innovation and co-creation methods. Why not include a specialist role such as **"innovation facilitator"** and let them create new and exciting collaborative experiences with and for your clients.

Legal designers in legal in-house departments and enterprises

In enterprises, the role of legal designers is different compared to in a law firm environment. One main reason for the different approach is the structure of large companies. Corporations are based on division of labor and have been consisting of different units such as management, finance, sales and distribution, marketing, IT, back office and more for much longer than law firms have. Law firms are just beginning to develop entrepreneurial structures, and are mostly still in the early stages of development. Of course, particularly in global law firms, there are already business units, but we should not forget that this is still a new tendency that has not yet had an impact on the entire industry.

In a company context, legal design aspects should be integrated early on in the development process, but also in the reorganization of legal departments and related contract departments. We therefore think that the right location for legal designers is in the area of legal departments – and there, in a new, cross-departmental position. Here, too, legal designers could be assigned such titles as **"head of legal customer success."** This job title should not be confused with employees working in marketing departments for customer satisfaction. The focus here is clearly on the word "legal." However, a close alignment and interaction between the two areas – general customer success and legal customer success – is highly recommended.

A legal designer could also take on the role of a **legal innovation facilitator,** thereby assisting the legal team to adopt more agile, client-centric ways of working. A legal designer might design and facilitate workshops and manage internal legal design projects to propel in-house legal innovation.

Conclusion

Legal designers in companies must be given an interface function in the area of innovation in law and be able to act on an equal footing with a general counsel. A legal designer should be able to move back and forth between the different areas and be given sufficient responsibility to ensure that their activities have an appropriate impact.

Reflections on the Role of the Legal Designer

Legal design is a completely new profession, and legal designers have yet to find the right role in the various legal organizations. We believe that the current situation, in which legal designers act more as external consultants, will change in the future. We believe that a permanent role in organizations will be important in order to really take advantage of the full spectrum of possibilities that legal design offers.

Collaboration and an open mindset are absolute prerequisites for this in all the units described. And if these basic prerequisites do not yet exist, the skill set of legal designers, as we have described in this book, is the ideal foundation for establishing and sustainably anchoring an innovative mindset in the legal context.

An exciting question, of course, is where the legal designers of the future can be trained for these positions. Here, too, we can observe that at the moment it is primarily the pioneers in legal design who are providing both advice and further training. However, we firmly believe that we need to institutionalize the education of legal designers in order to make access to those skills available in the first place. We are already in contact with universities and technical colleges. Who knows – maybe we will soon see a real legal design curriculum that will fully train and prepare legal designers for the abovementioned roles, professions and possibilities.

The desire for such programs reaches us daily. That was also one of the main reasons why we decided to write this book. We want to share our knowledge and make it accessible to other people so that they, too, can work as legal designers in the future.

(Relatively) New Roles In Law

Over the last couple of years, we can already observe a tremendous change in terms of more innovation-driven law firms that have added several new functions to the original team setup in recent years.

Marketing

This was one of the first changes in modern law firms. Adding marketing as a separate department is not as old as one might think.

Business development

More and more law firms have added a professional business development position and sometimes a team that supports lawyers in business issues, particularly in pitches. Most business development departments in law firms are part of the marketing section.

Legal tech

For quite some time we have observed legal tech specialists and sometimes even legal engineers among the employees in law firms.

Legal operations

Legal operations managers are one of the newbies among additional staff in law firms.

Innovation teams

Among law firms that are really ahead of the curve, we see more and more initiatives that call themselves "innovation teams."

Chapter 6
The Role of Legal Designers

Chapter 7
Legal User Experiences

7

Legal User Experiences

Chapter 7
Legal User Experiences

From the Traditional Legal Delivery Model to Legal User Experience (LUX)

There are several aspects that comprise the provision of quality legal services. From our perspective, the "legal quality" pyramid below effectively communicates the different tiers of quality:

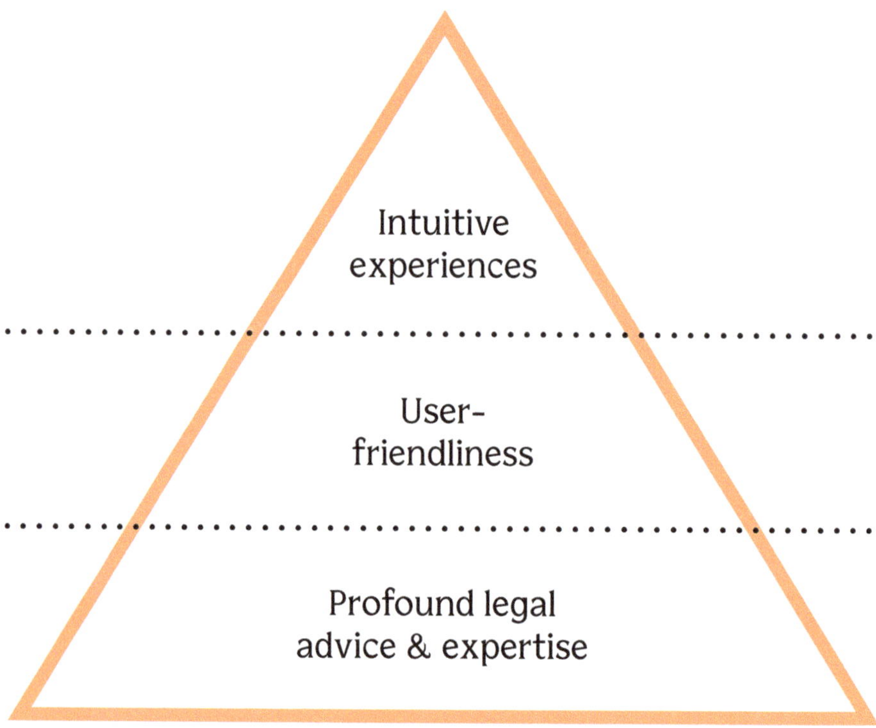

Tier 1: Foundation of profound legal advice and expertise

The basis of providing legal service is profound expert legal advice. This is the bare minimum in terms of quality. Clients expect clear terms and sound legal advice that minimizes any risks. For many years, performing and operating at the base of the pyramid alone was sufficient, but not anymore.

Now, in order to stand out from the crowd, lawyers must deliver at all tiers of the legal quality pyramid.

Tier 2: User-friendliness

The second tier of quality that we identify is the requirement to build user-friendly legal environments and services. For the first time, legal design can play a major role in developing solutions that are not only legally profound and safe but also user-friendly. As a result of the human-centric outlook advocated by legal design, legal services or content that are created using legal design skills are more likely to resonate with the actual user of a legal service and as such be deemed more user-friendly.

In recent times, we have observed that there has been greater adoption and recognition of the value of making legal services truly user-friendly. Accordingly, we have seen an increase in the number of legal teams challenging themselves to create user-centered legal solutions that deliver more than just profound legal advice.

Tier 3: Summit: Intuitive experiences

At the top of the pyramid are what we call intuitive experiences. An intuitive experience occurs when a user's interaction with a legal product or service does not feel legal, but rather familiar, and therefore intuitive.

Examples include:

- Easy-to-use legal tech platforms for flight or train delays, like Flightright, Aireclaim, MyRight, etc.[50]
- Smooth service that combines analogue and digital legal offerings, like easy-to-use legal templates on law firm websites or websites such as Legal Zoom.
- Basic legal questions answered free in real time, with a chatbot or a question-and-answer template solution. Take a look at Chevalier Rechtsanwälte or Clarius Legal.[51]
- In-house, we might find an app or an interface on other devices that assists salespeople in the organization in understanding the relevant legal obligations and finding answers to their legal and compliance questions in real time (for example, during a sales pitch to clients).
- Guiding people through legal content such as contracts in an intuitive way. This could be analogue or digital. We are continuously inspired by the new legal contracts, which do not look or feel like contracts at all. Companies such as Tony's Chocolonely, Airbus and National Australia Bank have all experimented with creating intuitive legal content.
- Non-coding tools for lawyers that enable them to create automated workflows or chatbots, like Bryter or Josef.[52]

As a result of the COVID-19 pandemic in 2020, we have also seen the rise of intuitive legal apps such as e-gree, an app that democratizes access to basic legal services for anyone with a smartphone. The app, which is backed by heavyweight investors such as supermodel Natalia Vodianova, allows people to quickly create legally sound contracts relating to jobs, ventures, prenups, uncoupling and wills in just three quick steps, all on your smartphone. Oh, and it's free, thereby promoting access to quality legal advice for all.

50 https://www.flightright.com/; https://aireclaim.com/; https://www.myright.de/

51 https://www.kanzlei-chevalier.de/; https://clarius.legal/

52 https://bryter.io/; https://joseflegal.com/

So how do you progress from the foundational quality level to the summit? Legal design is a tool to help legal providers take off from Tier 1 and achieve Tiers 2 and 3 to deliver a true legal user experience. The goal of a good user experience is to create a seamless, pleasantly flowing, intuitive and simple solution that enables a user to complete a certain task or reach a specific goal. A good user experience (and good service in general) consists of only a minimum number of steps, requires no prior knowledge of how to use the resource and works in a way that is familiar. A good experience will lead to a satisfied customer or client, because the service itself is helping them to achieve what they desired.[53]

What Makes a Good Legal User Experience?

Transferred to the legal world, a good legal user experience, or LUX, as we call it, consists of all three levels of quality: the delivery of watertight legal expert advice or guidance that is delivered in a user friendly manner and also leads the user through a smooth and pleasant journey, in an intuitive way, enabling them to feel legally safe and ideally equipped for their specific challenge. We encourage all legal professionals to use the three tiers in the legal quality pyramid as a benchmark to assess your current offerings and transform your services to offer a true legal user experience. We must look beyond colors and visuals and instead ask ourselves at each touchpoint in our offerings, "Are we creating an enjoyable and seamless experience for our users in any legal context?"

53 See also Downe, *Good Services.*

Chapter 7
Legal User Experiences

Chapter 8
The Value of Legal Design

8

The Value of Legal Design

Chapter 8
The Value of Legal Design

Legal design is a secret ingredient that will help you transform your traditional legal business into a business-driven and innovative, user-centric organization.

How can we measure the success and value of legal design?

This is one of the questions we are asked most often. Before we delve into ways of demonstrating the measurable value of legal design, let's first take a look at other industries and the value of design there.

As we have explored in previous chapters, design thinking is known to be one of the most successful innovation methods of our time. Almost all tools and intuitive products and services are based on this human-centered development method, whether they are mobile devices like the iPhone or food delivery services like Foodora.

The success of such products and services shows how effective design is as a business development factor. Several studies have demonstrated that companies that employ design as a core innovation driver to develop products and services in a user-oriented way exhibit increased performance by up to 211% compared to the time when design did not yet play a role.

According to the Design Management Institute (DMI), "the most innovative companies in the world share one thing in common. They use design as an integrative resource to innovate more efficiently and successfully. Yet many businesses don't make it a priority to invest in design – often because the value of design is hard to measure and define as a business strategy. The DMI

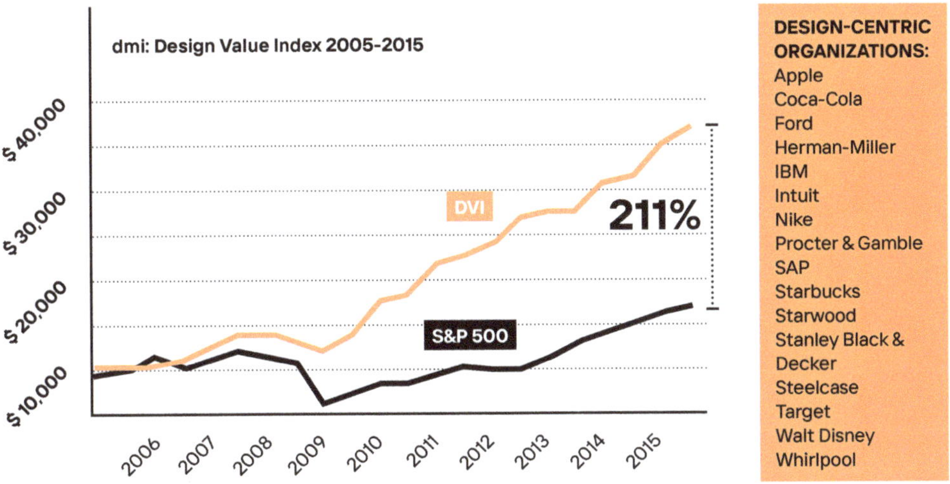

Source: Design Management Institute[54]

Design Value Index has taken the mystery out of measurement, demonstrating that an unequivocal financial advantage is attributable to those that do dare to make design a priority."[55]

This finding by the Design Management Institute (DMI) ought to be reason enough for the legal industry to invest in design as well. But we know that one study alone is not a convincing argument, particularly for lawyers.

So how can we be sure that legal design will have a similar impact on our industry?
Since we know the legal market from different perspectives and have been working in it for many years, we know that our profession in general still needs further guidance. Lawyers are usually not very fast when it comes to change and innovation. Only a detailed examination of the topic and a description of how to approach it in the legal industry will provide a basis for the necessary change.

54 Westcott, "Design-Driven Companies"

55 Westcott, "Design-Driven Companies"

Measuring the Value of Legal Design

In order to measure the impact of legal design initiatives (and thereby demonstrate their tangible value), legal ecosystems need to start moving towards a culture of data-driven decision-making and setting key performance indicators (KPIs) that align with their business objectives and strategies.

Data-driven decision-making

What does it mean to be data-driven?

Being "data-driven" means that a company makes strategic and business decisions based on data analysis and interpretation. It encompasses building tools and capabilities and at its core, a culture that acts on data as a primary driver of decision-making.

Legal ecosystems usually use facts and laws as the key bases for making decisions. However, with the exponential increase in legal technology and analytics in the legal sector, we advocate that all legal teams should be shifting gears to use data-driven decision-making to inform their strategies, goals, business plans and client service.

How to get started with data-driven legal design

If your team does not incorporate much (or any) data into its decision-making methods, it can feel somewhat daunting. The interesting thing is that becoming "data-driven" does not necessarily mean investing large sums of money into data analytics and software. It is more about taking a proactive approach to collecting data in numerous ways (and yes, some of these methods may utilize data analytics software). It is an ongoing commitment to adopting data-driven practices, and while it is initially difficult, the payoff is worth the effort. Trust us – you will certainly receive returns on your investment once you begin to harness the power of data.

Here are some first steps to get started towards your goal of becoming data-driven:

1. Start by analyzing your key existing clients. If you are part of a law firm, you could request access to your website analytics. See which articles get the most clicks, which country the most viewers are from, how long they stay on the website, whether any of them reach out to lawyers, or how long they stay on certain pages. If you don't have access to this data, then start by analyzing your existing customer behavior: How often do key customers call, email or text? What topics recur frequently? Which clients seem to be the most challenging? Which clients are recurring and pleasant? What are their distinguishing features? Collect this data and use it to then create user personas of your key clients. For more about user personas, see Chapter 4.
2. Conduct focus groups, surveys or interviews to obtain a robust 360-degree view of internal talent, clients and the business. Collate all the data in an Excel sheet or visualize it visualize it for example in a MS PowerBI dashboard and set up quarterly interviews to track changes in sentiments.
3. If you are trying out a product, such as a new legal technology, implement A/B user testing. You may need some assistance from your IT department; however, the analytics obtained from such testing will help you to quickly decide on the type of legal tech solution that fits your team and organization best.
4. Now that you're becoming comfortable with the act of collecting data to drive decisions, it's time to look for a good legal tech platform that will run the analytics for you, particularly when it comes to contracts.

Key Performance Indicators (KPIs)

What are KPIs?

A key performance indicator (KPI) is a measurable value that gauges a company's effectiveness. KPIs provide a way to see whether key business objectives are being achieved. KPIs can be used at almost every level and context of business to evaluate success and the achievement of targets.

Aligning KPIs to business objectives

A pitfall that is often faced when setting KPIs is that they are not aligned to a company's business objectives and strategy. In order to set the right KPIs, there needs to be close contact between members of the legal department and people in strategic decision-making roles. This would require those in strategic decision-making roles to ensure that the business strategy is communicated clearly and understood by all staff – including lawyers and in-house legal teams.

Business objectives might include aspects such as:

- Acquiring certain clients.
- Increasing efficiency in case matters.
- Moving towards digitalization.
- Increasing corporate social responsibility initiatives.

For example, in a large company, one business objective could be that all teams are to complete more tasks in-house (i.e., not brief out to external agencies, consultants or law firms). As an in-house lawyer, one solution you may have identified to reach this business objective is to onboard certain automation technology. A KPI that aligns with the business objectives would therefore be the percentage of the cost of external briefing that decreased due to onboarding legal technology. By aligning your KPIs firmly with your business objectives and strategy, you set yourself and your team up for success in the organization context.

So before setting your KPIs, be sure that your team has a thorough understanding of the key strategic objectives for the business. Then set the KPIs to align clearly with these strategic and business objectives.

KPIs in legal design

Key performance indicators in legal design work in two directions: classical parameters (as known from other business) and user satisfaction. In our daily practice, we regularly ask lawyers about the specific KPIs they would like to set for a given legal design project.

Quite often, the response is a slightly puzzled look, as if the lawyers are unsure of what KPIs to set. The hard truth is that the legal market lags far behind in measuring business outcomes with KPIs. Law firms are still mainly using the billable hour system to charge their clients, so in that respect they do measure the amount of time they invest in a case. But measuring the amount of time spent on certain workflows and processes, communication with suppliers, and repeating the same process again and again is not something that has been developed yet in the legal world. Actually, for private-practice lawyers, the billable hour is generally their only form of target or KPI – and this in itself directly contradicts the notion of increasing efficiency. More efficiency is less time billed, which ultimately leads to less revenue. We see that private-practice legal ecosystems in particular are designed to work against KPIs that are related to business efficiency goals.

In the arena of KPIs and measuring business value, we observe that in-house legal departments are more advanced than their private-practice contemporaries. However, even in this scenario, there is room for in-house legal departments to use KPIs on a broader scale in order to really highlight the value of their initiatives. That's why in this chapter we have decided to focus on and highlight ways that you can introduce KPIs effectively to drive your legal organization towards becoming a savvy business unit.

How to start

Before you can measure success, you need primary data with which you can later compare your results. Due to the situation in the legal market that we have described earlier, there is often no valid base of numbers, indicators or tasks available for making later comparisons.
So the first step in every organization is to start collecting data. This allows you to measure your success based on values before and after introducing a solution.

Below are some key indicators that are useful to think about when it comes to innovation in law. One remark from our end: Start today! Take a look around at your daily tasks and start defining the indicators that could be relevant. And then be honest with yourself! Begin to measure everything that appears interesting to you: the amount of time it takes to complete a certain task, the involvement of people and systems in a certain workflow, the time needed to read a certain contract or similar – anything you can think of that can be measured.

Evaluation process:

When measuring the success of a legal design project, make sure to set KPIs relating to your QUEs:

→ Quality: What kind of results were obtained? How accurate and reliable are the results?

→ User satisfaction: How did users respond? What feedback did you elicit?

→ Effectiveness: Speed, efficiency?

In addition to QUEs, reflect on the "soft factors" from your users. How did they feel through the project? Think about their frustration levels, friction levels, enjoyment levels. Which parts derived the most contentment, and where are the possibilities to improve in your next project?

Why are KPIs important?

KPIs are important for many reasons:

- You can measure as many different parameters as there are. This is important for your organization to see whether or not your change, project or innovation is a real business success.
- With tangible data, you can convince people to invest in innovation if you can show the effectiveness of using new solutions.
- The comparison of "before and after" data is often a mind-blowing realization for your organization.
- People love numbers and proof that certain things are working. If you set the right numbers, attributes and success indicators, you can help your organization to become more effective and invest only in solutions that are worth it.
- No KPI can work without the right measurement! Starting to collect data is very good, but don't forget to use the right evaluation techniques to measure your before and after values. In legal design projects, we conduct user testing in order to measure whether a newly created solution is as effective as intended (user-centered evaluation).

Types of KPIs in the context of legal design

So, you want to know what types of KPIs to set? Here are some of our favorites, which we often set with clients and collaborators:

To measure the efficiency of a contract:

- Volume of a specific contract (by how many pages has a document or template been reduced?)
- Reading time required for a document.
- How many times does the contract go back and forth between parties before finalization?
- What parts of the contract need further explanation or frequently lead to requests from the other party?
- Are there any patterns with regard to certain parts of a contract that often need more clarification?
- Are there any lessons from previous contracts that you should look at before turning to another contract?

To better understand client interaction:

- How many separate legal services do you offer to your clients (internally or externally)?
- How often do you conduct a survey with your clients?
- How often do you ask clients what they need?
- Is there a certain protocol for your organization to inquire about clients' satisfaction/needs before, during and after a certain legal service is delivered?
- Is there a standard protocol for what to do after providing a legal service (e.g., knowledge collection about specifics, where and when a document has to be stored, etc.)?
- How much time does each individual legal service take in your own organization?
- How much time does each individual legal service take in your client's

organization?

- How much time do you invest in general requests?
- How much time do you need for clarifications concerning legal documents?
- What parts of the legal service journey take the most time?
- How many persons and systems are involved in each legal service you offer to your clients?
- How much time do you need for negotiations with the client in general and concerning a specific task?
- Do you really know whether your client is happy with your offerings?

To measure the efficiency of processes

- How many contracts/templates does your organization provide/deal with?
- How many different contracts/documents are you generally working on?
- How many specific contracts/documents exist?
- How many standard documents are you using?
- What tasks need to be completed in order to deliver a certain service (how many steps do you need to provide a service)?
- Is there a standard process for specific tasks implemented?
- Do people have a clear structure for how to handle diverse requests?
- How many approvals does a document/legal service need?
- How many persons are involved in the process from beginning to end?
- Who has what questions? Analyze the quality of requests in the context of the document and find patterns.
- Measure the time from the start of a process to end, when a document is signed.
- What does the document journey look like?

Demonstrating the Value of Legal Design

In summary, how can you demonstrate the value of legal design to the business?

Start collecting data and use data to inform decision-making.
Start to find like-minded people in your organization, who are ready to innovate.
Determine a strategy for implementing legal design.
Start with a (small) pilot case and measure the results. This can be a use case to influence the business to keep investing in legal design.
Measure the before and after results when using legal design as a method.
Show the results to decision-makers.
Obtain feedback after legal design workshops and education sessions.
Hire an external legal design expert to help you establish legal design within your organization.
Create an innovation journey story and share it with the business. Do not underestimate the power of storytelling as a tool to sell and convince others.

The Impact of Legal Design: Short-Term, Mid-Term and Long-Term

Short-term: after a first legal design project you will...

Get a first tangible result.
Can start measuring your KPIs in the context of a legal design project.
Start true collaboration and building an understanding of your audience.
Start equipping yourself with legal design methods for the future.
Have a starting point for a flexible, changing and open-minded culture.
Have an innovative initiative to show internally and externally.

Mid-term: after 12 months of adopting legal design initiatives you will...

Start to gain traction and wider adoption.
Re-design your organization towards a more innovative culture.
Increase the empowerment of people.
Discover cost savings.
Realize return on your investment.
Have simpler workflows and more efficient processes.
Create easier-to-access legal content.
Create better contracts and negotiation interactions.

Long-term: when legal design is an embedded way of working, you will...

Become a cost-effective, innovative, user-centric organization.
Notice a shift towards collaborative working and open growth mindsets.
Reposition legal professionals as innovators.
Establish dynamic and agile teams that are open to fast-paced change.

Chapter 8

The Value of Legal Design

Conclusion →

Conclusion

Conclusion

We have taken you on a practical and hopefully illustrative journey through terrain that is still unfamiliar to many: we showed you the land of innovation in law through the lens of legal design.

If you have read the book up to this point, you should now have a very good overview and a clearer understanding of topics such as design, design thinking and, of course, legal design in all its dimensions and implications.

Ideally, we hope that our book encourages you to be bold and curious, to explore and to approach making improvements in the future with a new perspective. Embrace change – it is not to be feared. Remember to be eager to embrace a new mindset, work together with other disciplines, tap into the power of legal design and begin to measure success with our practical KPI guideline.

If there is one thing that we have learned in our own consulting work, it is that legal design in practice is, above all, a lot of fun!

It is incredibly satisfying each time we work together with various clients from law firms, legal departments or institutions:

→ To jointly solve a problem.
→ To establish and enhance collaborative and co-creative ways of working.
→ To untie a knot that existed.
→ To observe how participating team members grow through working on such tasks.

For us, this is our greatest reward – sharing such feelings of success and making our small contribution to improving access to law, teaching others about user-centeredness and creativity so that they too possess useful tools that make it easier for people to understand and use law intuitively.

We're glad you've read our book, and we are always happy to receive your feedback, questions and suggestions.

Let's work together to grow the legal design profession – there can't be enough of our kind!

With best regards,

Astrid Kohlmeier & Meera Klemola

Astrid Kohlmeier

Author

Astrid Kohlmeier is a lawyer and internationally renowned legal design pioneer. She has been combining law and design for more than 15 years, with senior roles in the insurance-, litigation finance- and service design industries. The legal design expert advises legal inhouse departments and law firms such as Clifford Chance, Linklaters, Airbus, SAP, NetApp and many more. Winner of several design awards as well as honoured as "woman of legal tech", she develops user-centric legal solutions with a focus on innovation and digital transformation. Astrid is a member and lecturer of the Executive Faculty at the Bucerius Center on the Legal Profession, co-founder of the non-profit organization "Liquid Legal Institute e.V.", speaker at relevant conferences worldwide and works with a global network of legal designers. She is actively engaged at the intersection of education and method development to establish the profession of " legal designers" worldwide.

Meera Klemola

Author

Meera Klemola is globally recognised as one of the pioneering voices in Human Centred Design for legal professionals and legal business. Dubbed by The Legal Forecast as one of the first 'Legal Designers' and the host of the world's first Legal Design Summit, Meera continues to lead and actively contribute to the discourse on the evolving role of design in law as well as corporate learning and development. Meera is a trusted advisor to some of the largest brands, corporations, law firms and in-house legal teams. She also co-teaches with professors at law schools, is a frequently requested keynote speaker at global innovation conferences and company retreats and is a contributing author to various platforms on the topics of design in law, modern work and leadership. She holds multidisciplinary qualifications in law, design management and business.

Legal design from the book designer's perspective

I am a freelance designer and thinker working with agencies and companies alike. Usually, I'm involved in anything loosely along the lines of branding, UI, UX, concept development, strategy and human-centered design. In this case I had the honor of laying out the book in front of you.

When I first heard of a thing called legal design I have to admit that I was a little bewildered. Law and design were not a pairing that would have come to my mind when looking for interesting fields of work. In fact, if it weren't for Astrid I might have never heard the term at all.

But looking into the subject a little deeper the topic seemed intriguing. My background is in design, mostly what you would call graphic design, with a growing share of design thinking and more theoretical or systematic approaches. Law to me was (and frankly still is) a necessity to achieve clarity or protection, likely when things go wrong. There is a somewhat negative connotation to all things „law". Clearly, I am biased and prejudiced when it comes to legal matters. Though, I did always have a soft spot for texts and the beauty of a well formed sentence. Certainly an aid in what was to come. After all, legal design did open up a completely new perspective to me.

Who would have thought a designer could have fun working on legal documents. With lawyers.

To me, reworking things for readability and style isn't a new concept. But legal texts? If you had asked me two years ago I couldn't have named a thing further away from readability and style.

But I was curious. When it came to user agreements and NDAs – things that I am actually confronted with myself on a daily basis – the premise of legal design was clear and grand, immediately.
Diving into material, analyzing and reworking it bit by bit turns out to be a fun challenge every time. And the benefit of my work is visible almost instantly. I hope I can bring a good set of skills to the table, not only as a designer, but also as a potential user.

If there is at least one user I can help understand what they are looking at, my work is done well. And if there is at least one lawyer who I can help to understand what their user is looking for, my work is done better.

Here I am. Having fun working
on legal documents.
With lawyers.

Tobias Heumann
Designer

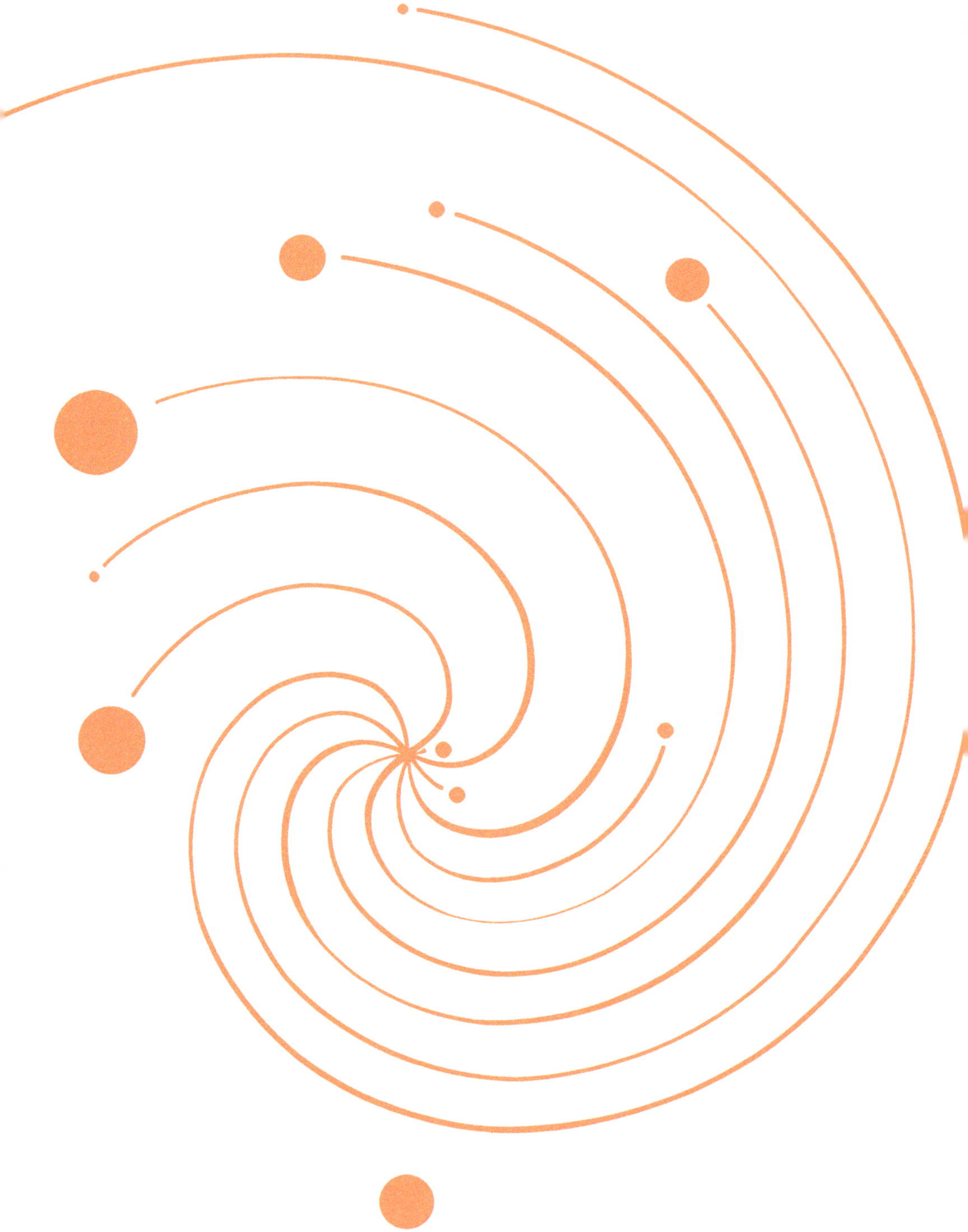

Space for Thoughts

⟵ Conclusion

Bibliography →

Bibliography

Chapter 1

Kelley, Tom and David Kelley. *Creative Confidence: Unleashing the Creative Potential within Us All.* New York: Crown Business, 2013.

Nielsen, Dorte, and Sarah Thurber. *The Secret of the Highly Creative Thinker*. Amsterdam: BIS Publishers, 2016.

Wired.com (blog); "Kevin Kelly and Steven Johnson on Where Ideas Come From," posted September 27, 2010. https://www.wired.com/2010/09/mf-kellyjohnson/

Edmondson, Amy, Psychological Safety and Learning Behavior in Work Teams," *Administrative Science Quarterly* 44, no. 2 (June 1999). https://web.mit.edu/curhan/www/docs/Articles/15341_Readings/Group_Performance/Edmondson%20Psychological%20safety.pdf

re:Work (blog); "The Five Keys to a Successful Google Team" by Julia Rozovsky, posted November 17, 2015. https://rework.withgoogle.com/blog/five-keys-to-a-successful-google-team/

Chapter 2

Legal Geek/Legal Design Geek Conference: https://www.legalgeek.co.

Mellinkoff, David. *The Language of the Law*. Boston: Little, Brown, 1963.

Brunschwig, Colette R. *Visualisierung von Rechtsnormen: Legal Design*. Zurich: Schulthess Juristische Medien, 2001.

Legal Design Jam: http://legaldesignjam.com/

Cox, George. *Cox Review of Creativity and Business: Building on the UK's Strengths*. London: Design Council, 2005.

Sullivan, Louis H. *The Tall Office Building Artistically Considered*. Philadelphia: J.B. Lippincott, 1896.

Kries, Mateo, and Jolanthe Kugler. *The Bauhaus #itsalldesign*. Exhibition catalogue. Weil am Rhein, Germany: Vitra Design Museum, 2015.

Senge, Peter. *The Fifth Discipline: The Art & Practice of the Learning Organization*. New York: Doubleday, 1990.

Martin, Roger. *The Design of Business*. Brighton, Massachusetts: Harvard Business School Press, 2009.

Kolko, Jon. *Thoughts on Interaction Design*, 2nd ed. Burlington, Massachusetts: Morgan Kaufmann, 2011.

Interaction Design Foundation (blog); "Interaction Design." https://www.interaction-design.org/literature/topics/interaction-design

Brown, Tim, ed. *IDEO Design Thinking* (blog). https://designthinking.ideo.com/blog

Chapter 3

DeStefano, Michele. *Legal Upheaval: A Guide to Creativity, Collaboration, and Innovation in Law*. Chicago: American Bar Association, 2018.

Cohen, Mark A., "What Does 'More With Less' Mean For The Legal Industry?", *Forbes*, August 6, 2019, https://www.forbes.com/sites/markcohen1/2019/08/06/what-does-more-with-less-mean-for-the-legal-industry/?sh=6000399f5c2f

Thomson Reuters, *2019 Law Firm Business Leaders Report*, 2019, https://images.thomsonreuters.com/Web/TRlegalUS/%7Bb702578c-1d7d-42df-8d67-348e5a31289e%7D_Law_Firm_Leaders_Final_10.17.19_print.pdf

Veith, Christian, Nora Tophof, Tessia Tober, Meinhard Weizmann, Markus Hartung and Dirk Hartung. *Legal Operations: Getting More from In-House Legal Departments and Their Outside Counsel*. Boston Consulting Group/Bucerius Law School, 2018. https://www.law-school.de/fileadmin/content/law-school.de/de/units/abt_education/pdf/Studien/Report_Legal_Operations_Bucerius_BCG.pdf

Susskind, Richard. *Online Courts and the Future of Justice.* Oxford: Oxford University Press, 2019.

Brown, Tim. *Change by Design, Revised and Updated: How Design Thinking Transforms Organizations and Inspires Innovation.* New York: Harper Business, 2019

Nicholas Carr, "'The Shallows': This is Your Brain Online," interview by Robert Siegel, All Things Considered, NPR, June 2, 2010, https://www.npr.org/templates/story/story.php?storyId=127370598&t=1610479712659&t=1615042598741

Olson, Elizabeth, "Judges Push Brevity in Briefs, and Get a Torrent of Arguments," *The New York Times,* October 3, 2016, https://www.nytimes.com/2016/10/04/business/dealbook/judges-push-brevity-in-briefs-and-get-a-torrent-of-arguments.html

CNIL (Commission Nationale de l'Informatique et des Libertés), "The CNIL's restricted committee imposes a financial penalty of 50 Million euros against GOOGLE LLC," CNIL website, January 21, 2019, https://www.cnil.fr/en/cnils-restricted-committee-imposes-financial-penalty-50-million-euros-against-google-llc

Kohlmeier, Astrid, and Joaquin Santuber, Is the Common Legal Platform a Wicked Problem? A Legal Design Approach and Case Study," in *Liquid Legal: Towards a Common Legal Platform,* eds. Kai Jacob, Dierk Schindler and Roger Strathausen. Cham, Switzerland: Springer Nature Switzerland, 2020.

Wolters Kluwer, "Future Ready Lawyer 2020," Wolters Kluwer website, 2020, https://info.wolterskluwer.de/future-ready-lawyer-2020#

Chapter 4

Gaver, William, Tony Dunne and Elena Pacenti, "Design: Cultural Probes," *ACM Interactions,* vol. 1 (January/February 1999), 21–29, https://interactions.acm.org/archive/view/jan.-feb.-1999/design-cultural-probes1

Robson, Rick E, "Building a Useful Research Tool: An Origin Story of AEIOU," Epic website,

posted February 23, 2015,
https://www.epicpeople.org/building-a-useful-research-tool/

What Makes Lawyers Tick (blog); "The Lawyer Personality: Why Lawyers Are Skeptical" by Dr. Larry Richard, posted February 11, 2013,
https://www.lawyerbrainblog.com/2013/02/the-lawyer-personality-why-lawyers-are-skeptical/
Nielsen, Dorte, and Sarah Thurber. *The Secret of the Highly Creative Thinker.* Amsterdam: BIS Publishers, 2016.
[Source also cited in Chapter 1]

Both, Thomas, and Nadia Roumani. *Ideation/Creation Expedition: A flight plan for design exploration.* Designing for Social Systems, Stanford d.school, vol. 2 (August, 2019),
https://static1.squarespace.com/static/57c6b79629687fde090a0fdd/t/5d98057f6684440c91591c0c/1570243968564/Ideation-Expedition-Flight-Plan-Aug-2019-V2.pdf

"Brainwriting: Enabling Everyone to Share Their Creative Ideas," Mind Tools (website), https://www.mindtools.com/pages/article/newct_86.htm

Medium.com (blog), "How|Now|Wow (Ciao!)" by Joelle Hagen, posted September 7, 2020,
https://medium.com/@joellewhagen/how-now-wow-ciao-2241cf6d6314

Brown, Tim. *Change by Design, Revised and Updated: How Design Thinking Transforms Organizations and Inspires Innovation.* New York: Harper Business, 2019

Chapter 5

"Innovation," Clifford Chance website,
https://www.cliffordchance.com/hubs/innovation-and-best-delivery-hub/innovation-and-best-delivery.html

"Ten Pitfalls to Avoid in Contracting," World Commerce & Contracting website,
https://www.worldcc.com/Resources/Content-Hub/View/ArticleID/3972

Chapter 6

Connor, Peter, "The T-Shaped Lawyer," Legal Business World website, posted December 22, 2017, https://www.legalbusinessworld.com/post/2017/12/22/the-t-shaped-lawyer

Hansen, Morten T., "IDEO CEO Tim Brown: T-Shaped Stars: The Backbone of IDEO's Collaborative Culture," Chief Executive website, posted January 21, 2010, https://chiefexecutive.net/ideo-ceo-tim-brown-t-shaped-stars-the-backbone-of-ideoaes-collaborative-culture__trashed/

Carrel, Alyson, and Caitlin Moon, "The Delta Model," Design Your Delta website, https://www.designyourdelta.com/

"Design Thinking Mindset for Innovation," Hasso-Plattner-Institut website, https://hpi-academy.de/design-thinking/design-thinking-mindset-for-innovation.html

Chapter 7

Downe, Louise. *Good Services: How to Design Services that Work*. Amsterdam: BIS Publishers, 2020.

Chapter 8

Westcott, Michael, "Design-Driven Companies Outperform S&P by 228% over Ten Years – The 'DMI Design Value Index,'" DMI: Design Management Institute website, March 10, 2014, https://www.dmi.org/blogpost/1093220/182956/Design-Driven-Companies-Outperform-S-P-by-228-Over-Ten-Years--The-DMI-Design-Value-Index

Images & Illustrations

Schelte Adams Bolswert after Sir Peter Paul Rubens, "Lion Hunt,"
47.4 x 65 cm, engraving, Ailsa Mellon Bruce Fund, Open Access image, National Gallery of Art, Wahsington, D.C., USA, accessed 13 May 2021,
https://www.nga.gov/collection/art-object-page.54063.html

after Winslow Homer, “Jurors Listening to Counsel, Supreme Court, New City Hall, New York,” wood engraving, Print Purchase Fund (Rosenwald Collection), Open Access image, National Gallery of Art, Wahsington, D.C., USA, accessed 13 May 2021, https://www.nga.gov/collection/art-object-page.45619.html

Greg Dlubacz, various Illustrations, accessed 13 May 2021 https://gregdlubacz.com/

Nadia Bormotova, opening page Illustrations, accessed 21 May 2021 https://www.istockphoto.com/de/portfolio/nadia_bormotova

Chapter 5, case study images courtesy of the respective authors if not specified

⟵ Bibliography

Index →

Index

Index of key words

Below is a list of the key words we have used throughout the book and where to find them.

www.ingramcontent.com/pod-product-compliance
Lightning Source LLC
Chambersburg PA
CBHW041304210926
51851CB00002B/8
9789529447251

Thank you for reading

The Legal Design Book

by Astrid Kohlmeier & Meera Klemola.

www.legaldesign-book.com